c.3

Am I still visible?

DATE DUE		
JAN 17 '84	JUL 1 1985	FEB 2 5 1991
FEB 06 '84	OCT 21 1985	1 1 1991
FEB 16 '84	NOV 28 1985	FEB 2 6 1992
	MAR 21 1986	DEC 0 3 1992
MAR 15 84	NOV 14 '86	JUL 1 1993
APR 13 84		
APR 23 84	FEB 02 '87	JAN 1 2 1996
JUN 14 90	MAR 0 2 1989	FEB 0 9 1996
DEC 1 0 1994		
FEB 12	NOV 1 3 1990	Feb 23
	JAN 16 '90	SEP 1 8 1996
MAR 2 85	FEB 27 199	DEC 0 1 1998
MAY 13 1985	Mar 14, 199	NOV 27 2000

INVOS

AM
I
STILL
VISIBLE?

AM I STILL VISIBLE?

A Woman's Triumph over Anorexia Nervosa

SANDRA H. HEATER

WHITE HALL BOOKS
Betterway Publications, Inc.
White Hall, Virginia

First Printing: May, 1983

WHITE HALL BOOKS are published and distributed by
Betterway Publications, Inc.
White Hall, Virginia 22987

Cover design by Barbara Wallace
Typography by Typecasting

Library of Congress Cataloging in Publication Data

Heater, Sandra Harvey
  Am I still visible?

  Bibliography: p.
  1. Anorexia nervosa.   I. Title.
RC552.A5H4   1983   616.85′2   83-6902
ISBN 0-932620-51-5
ISBN 0-932620-50-7 (pbk.)

Printed in the United States of America

*To all who have ever suffered
the wounds of anorexia
and especially to my family whose
steadfast support and love allowed me
to become visible at last.*

Foreword

As I begin to write this I am acutely aware that it is very late. I have just arrived home from the clinic where I spent the day in therapy working with depressed and desperate women, victims of anorexia nervosa and bulimia, individuals enslaved by their preoccupation with food and weight loss. These are women whose obsessions drive them to the very brink of madness—madness of such magnitude that loss of career, family, and even life may not detour them from their course of self-imposed destruction.

Each new day the phone rings with greater frequency. As I answer it is now common to be greeted by a small, desperate voice requesting help. With each new day I am repeatedly reminded of Sandra Heater's story and the importance of this book.

Sandra's story is important for several reasons. First, she typifies much that is held in high regard by society—bright, attractive, hard-working, high achievement, responsible citizen, etc. Her upbringing was middle class, like most of us. Her successes and failures are events we can relate to—wanting to please parents as a youngster, striving for peer recognition as an adolescent, struggling with deeply entrenched values as they clash with strong and undeniable feelings of young adulthood. And finally, as a young parent and wife, always trying to please and "do what is right." Her parents and family are good middle class people. In short, Sandra's life is much like most of our lives. However, there is something different about Sandra Heater. The very attributes that would ensure most of us success paradoxically become liabilities for her, pushing her into the dark abyss of anorexia nervosa.

Another important feature of Sandra's story is that she developed anorexia nervosa as an adult. This contrasts with the general thinking that the problem occurs primarily in the 12–18 year old age group. It is important in that it represents a phenomenon that appears to be becoming more pervasive. This disorder is spreading among those who are 25 to 45 years of age...even older. Sandra's thorough recall of her early life, and at times her excruciating introspection, is a remarkable effort in describing development of her potentially fatal disorder. Descriptions of family, friends, situations, and of herself are remarkably similar to the accounts heard again and again by those who are afflicted. While no book could hope to blueprint the dynamics of anorexia nervosa, this book provides guidelines, description, and general characteristics frequently associated with the development of anorexia nervosa. It serves as a valuable source of information for parents, friends, spouses, and the afflicted individual.

Sandra's story is most important because it represents hope for many individuals. Because she teetered precariously at the brink of insanity of self-imposed starvation and pulled away to pursue other goals of life and happiness, her story is clearly one of success. Her story is very real. It is not Cinderella-like for she sometimes still struggles intermittently with the subtle temptations of anorexia nervosa. Perhaps she will forever.

Sandra's story is a beacon of light and hope for those who feel trapped in the darkened and often hopeless world of anorexia nervosa. By sharing with others, there is no doubt she has increased the possibility of preventing or reducing suffering.

Last, this book is an important work in that Sandra has done a remarkable job of assembling a vast amount of relevant literature and theory, summarizing, and translating highly technical language into an understandable context for those who wish to know more about this most perplexing disorder. It describes with clarity how one of the most sustaining of all life's necessities becomes an enemy of the afflicted. It describes methodology of treatment and it offers family, friends, and those afflicted guidelines on how to proceed toward the resolution of this disabling disorder.

I believe Sandra's story will help many. But, in the final analysis, if her successful struggle to overcome the ravages of anorexia nervosa will help just one prospective victim, the value of this work unquestionably will have been validated.

> *Dr. Dan Baker*
> *Assistant Professor of Medical Psychology*
> *University of Nebraska Medical Center*

Contents

Prologue

The joyous Christmas Eve Mass had ended. As the pipe organ pealed out the final exultant strains of "Joy to the World," the congregation gathered to exchange Christmas greetings.

Apart from the happy milling crowd stood a woman alone. She waited expectantly for someone to stop and chat, but no one did. These long-time friends and acquaintances were uneasy, uncomfortable in approaching her, for how does one address the living dead?

Across the room her young husband eyed her in disbelief. If he felt an ice water shock each time he saw her, how must others react after a span of time?

This time last year, in fact only months ago, she had been a vivacious, healthy, lovely young woman, a former beauty contest winner who drew appreciative stares everywhere. And now she was an aged crone, emaciated and skeletal, stooped and pathetic.

He was at once moved to aching sorrow and to near revulsion. To think that this suffering was self-induced—it was almost more than he could bear. Obviously she was waiting in vain for the easy exchange of the other parishioners; it was time to rescue her and lead her home in the beginning hour of this Christmas morning. He could help her out of being covertly stared at and ignored, but he could not free her from the morass of her illness. Only she could conquer this bizarre scourge. He wondered whether she would ever find the strength to battle her illness.

She was struggling with *anorexia nervosa*, an insidious silent agony that causes its victims to starve themselves to death.

I know what this monster can do to the sufferer and her family, because I *am* that woman on that lonely Christmas Eve.

My story could be that of so many other anorexics, however. Perhaps in relating what happened to me, I can help awaken others to the course of this illness. Perhaps in my hard-won triumph, others may find encouragement when they need it most.

"I am," I said
To no one there,
But no one heard it at all,
Not even a chair.
—Neil Diamond, "I Am I Said

PART I
In The Beginning

Chapter 1

Back, back into the beginning, at least to the beginning of my life. One should go back much further, of course, to the very roots of one's existence, because we are part and parcel of all that preceded our being. Still it is enough to start from April 29, 1942, my birthday.

For reasons inexplicable even to her, my mother insisted on having me at home, attended only by a physician-friend and his wife, a registered nurse. It is surprising that a 36-year-old woman would choose this birthing situation but she did, and I arrived without complications into a welcoming family.

My older sister Louise had been a blond, curly-haired cherubic baby awash with dimples and smiles. What a contrast I presented with my exotic Oriental appearance, unfriendliness to all but my mother, and a decided tendency not to sleep.

Louise generously designated me a treasured sister and toy instead of a nuisance intruding in her fourteen-year-old life. She encouraged my development in every way and exulted in my early speech and apparent brightness.

Nursery pictures reveal me as a bald, chubby baby, somber and pensive-looking. I remember that during childhood I used to compare my baby pictures with those of my golden sister and was ashamed that my belly hung over my diapers.

One childish misinterpretation concerned me from very early on. My great-grandmother had been a heavy woman. She had died long before my birth, but I had seen her pictures. She definitely had been fat. She was also a successful business woman and extremely intelligent.

Once at a family gathering it was remarked that I reminded the elders of my great-grandmother. Immediate assurances that it was a similarity of personality and intellect, not a physical one, did little to dispel my repugnance. I did not want to resemble a rotund forebear in any way. Even then I thought fat was ugly.

[15]

As a young child I was strong-willed, adamant, resistant to disorder or change. My parents sold the family home when I was not quite two in order to buy and restore a large older home before the birth of their third daughter. Etched within my early memories is the disarray of remodeling, which to my infantile mind seemed hopeless. I sensed the disruption of routine and I did not like it at all.

Sarah, the third and last child of the family, arrived when I was just over two. Immediately she became "my" baby to be ferociously guarded and extravagantly loved.

Our childhood was comfortable, secure, and respectable. Adult roles were clearly defined, or so it seemed. Daddy made the living and Mother ran the house. Now, of course, I realize that there were subtle overlappings, but it all seemed so clear-cut back then. The household functioned around my father's schedule. He dairied, which imparted a certain diurnal and seasonal pattern.

Every June my mother's incipient wanderlust *almost* overcame her, but she refused to consider taking a trip on her own. She did what she felt she must and I observed.

I think that my parents always awed me just a bit. They were so reasonable, so mature that we rarely observed displays of temper or witnessed scenes of any sort. They were adults, the authority figures. I never questioned that authority or rebelled against it. Not overtly anyway.

Like other girls destined to become anorexic, as research now has shown, I had trouble accepting any imperfection in my parents. Because they seemed always right, I depended on them to formulate my own feelings. Like other anorexics I lacked the ability to trust my own emotions.

It is a painful process to scrutinize one's family beneath the microscope to see what interactions fed the development of an anorexic child. Memories become inaccurate, hazy, subject to the misinterpretations of time. Relying on questionable memories of childhood happiness and expecting perfect recall is a questionable process. How can I be fair in looking so far back to say that certain events probably caused my anorexia? Yet such introspection is necessary if an anorexic is to understand some basis for her disease and learn to trust her own view of life. If I am to become a visible person in my own eyes, I must try to see why I struggled desperately to vanish. I have tried to analyze our family structure and can only make some observations, clouded after thirty years. It seems that I patterned myself almost consciously after my father while clinging to my mother for security. Neither modeling nor dependence are conducive to developing a sound self-concept.

I never underwent psychoanalysis, and so I do not presume to guess why I was a "Mama's baby." Not every infant who clings to her mother becomes anorexic, of course. I do know that from one month old I abhorred separation from my mother and clung tenaciously to her. Did she encourage it? I don't remember, but I suspect not. After all, she had another child, a teenager; she had a busy social life, a husband closely involved with her. Knowing my mother as I do, I cannot believe that she would have tried to establish such unusually tight bonding.

I think back to those early days and wonder about my eating habits, because Bruch and other researchers believe that the anorexic has not been taught to differentiate true hunger from other sensations. Feeding was difficult during the first three months of my life. The formula disagreed with my system and I was highly allergic to the Karo in the milk. The problems were severe, but they were corrected within three months. One must remember that forty years ago pediatrics was not as sophisticated as it is now. But did this early problem contribute to my becoming anorexic? It is only a strand in the warp of the later illness.

My father was my model. He was dark and I am dark. He was reserved and I am self-contained. He was rational and I pride myself on being so. My paternal grandmother called me Little Richard and I remember how proud I was to be like my tall, strong father. I even have the "Harvey walk," a gait that lopes across the ground and conquers territory. We have places to go but rarely people to see. My father was not a "people person," preferring family and a few close friends to a crowd. My mother was the opposite. I chose my father's way. He had also been an excellent athlete in high school and college. Did someone speculate aloud or did I just infer that he would have liked a son to keep up the athletic tradition? On summer evenings after the milking chores were done, my father and my older male cousin popped flies and seemed to enjoy that a lot. Often I observed from the edge, not asking to play.

I know I tried to be my father's son to compensate for what I was convinced he missed. Yet we heard steadfast denial on his part that he had wanted sons instead of three daughters. To this day I do not know whether I perceived subtle nuances and internalized them, or instead simply made incorrect inferences and acted upon misinformation.

When I was growing up, a girl had a hard time developing her athletic prowess. Now girls are coming into their own, with Title IX and public opinion nudging girls' sports into prominence and respectability. My own daughter competes in three sports without compromising her femaleness. But in my small town when I was growing up, girls were girls. Period. Not that I had athletic talent; in fact, I probably did not. But I do remember the joy of running free, of horseback riding, of playing basketball and most of all, of trying to be a tomboy to make my father feel better. The sad part is that I don't believe he needed to be made to feel better.

He was a perfectionist and a self-driver. Some of the strongest memories of my childhood emanate from seeing my father come in from a hay field, so thin and gaunt and sweaty. He would drink quarts of iced tea. As if it were yesterday I can see the tall glass and hear the clink of the spoon against the ice as he stirred in the sugar. My mother worried about the way my father worked, that he was so thin, that he "overdid." I felt guilty that he was out there working so we could live so well. In retrospect, I wonder whether he could have worked less hard. I doubt it. I think that the same internal taskmaster drove him, and later drove me. He put up hay in the blistering sun, and I felt the same compulsion later on, in the physically taxing experience of anorexia.

My father seemed both strong and frail at the same time, someone to lean on and someone to protect. We kidded him about his harem and we waited on him in little ways, perhaps to appease the guilt for his labor. My mother almost always made biscuits for breakfast and we girls served them to him two at a time to assure a constant hot supply. Daddy could eat prodigious amounts and never gain an ounce. If I had inherited his crooked tooth and propensity for colds, why couldn't I have his metabolism too?

There was always so much dignity about my father. He loved us dearly, that I knew, but it was a gentle, proper love, not the roughhouse, give-and-take of some fathers and daughters. He was older when Sarah and I were born, well past forty. Younger parents are more prone to tumble on the floor with their kids. My father treated us with the dignity of an older parent.

Despite my parents' efforts to be generous, I had a hard time receiving gifts. Now I have learned that most anorexics are uncomfortable when gifts are given, believing themselves to be unworthy. Even in childhood I was a tough customer to buy for, rarely expressing a want. I was again patterning myself after my father, who impressed me as an almost ascetic individual.

Our family rarely dined out. A small town does not have many restaurants, but even if there had been some, I suspect we would not have gone often. On the rare occasions that we did eat out, my father would order frugally, even though he was generous with his family.

I make these observations in retrospect, in an effort to understand why I became anorexic. Whatever the ramifications of my patterning after my father, the fact is that we loved each other deeply and I miss him enduringly.

Another childhood influence was my grandmother, considered to be a beautiful woman. Once I visited an elderly friend of the family who told me that I looked just like Sarah Ellen. How pleased I was to look like my grandmother. I only knew her late in her life, when she was in ill health. She seemed to be the smallest adult I had ever known. I had often been told that she was beautiful and it never occurred to me that her beauty had faded with old age and illness. To me she was still beautiful, and *very* small. Did I make the faulty equation then between her tiny size and her beauty? These are musings recollected not in Wordsworthian tranquility but in the aftermath of upheaval.

When I was five, Louise went away to college. Three years later, in June, 1950, she married. I was crushed by both events and I felt with the occasional intuition of a child that her life was growing apart from mine. I missed her! Some years later she and her family moved back to our home town and we were able to reconfirm early emotional bonds.

What was growing up like in a small heart-of-America town in the late 1940s and '50s? At the time I could not imagine any other sort of life. We lived snugly, comfortably on a tree-lined street. My parents had a large circle of friends and often entertained, but my mother was the real socializing force in the family.

Those were the days of sit-down dinner parties with thank-you calls as the proper follow-up the next day. Our house was attractive, since Mother is a natural interior decorator with an innate sense of color, balance, and subdued drama. She is a splendid cook and arranger of flowers; she overwhelmed me then and ever afterward with her menus and centerpieces. I delighted in watching her create beauty and longed to emulate that talent but alas, could not. My role was that of willing helper. She arranged the flower beds and I carried little pails of water, handing her the plants and tools. My sister and I learned early the correct way to set a table. I well remember standing at one end of the dining table and eyeing the place settings to check their alignment. No one ever saw a bottle or jar on our table to disturb the beauty of the inevitable centerpiece. We were completely proper people, as our dining ceremonies reflected. Our eating habits did not go to the extreme of ritual, a family pattern sometimes associated with anorexia nervosa. But food preparation and serving were important to Mother and her helpers.

The most memorable traumas associated with meal times concerned my younger sister. Until she was three Sarah was the happiest, bubbly baby imaginable. Then she broke her leg and became almost frail. She ate little, from a limited list of foods she liked. My parents cajoled, bribed, and threatened to get her to eat. I hated the tension at the dining table, but more important I was furious at anything that made Sarah unhappy. If she didn't want to eat, that was fine with me. Why didn't my parents agree? Surreptitiously I slipped food from her plate and ate it myself, to make it appear that Sarah had eaten more. For a period of two or three years there were intermittent battles between my parents and my little sister. And our family pediatrician only intensified the struggle to get Sarah to eat more.

These episodes in my memory reveal several things. First, *not* eating was getting prolonged attention. Secondly, I remember helplessness. I could not soothe Sarah, so I suppressed my childish anger, having no means to strike back—at least not then. Later, was I using anorexia as a way of retaliating for offenses against my beloved little sister?

The ceremonies at our dining table continued to be important to me. I made out tally cards for bridge parties and soon knew to serve from the left and remove from the right. I thoroughly enjoyed doing all these things. Their order and structure comforted, and having social skills made growing up infinitely easier in many ways. I never felt uncomfortable or intimidated by circumstances or people, so long as those people were adults.

Grown-ups were easy to be with: interesting, settled, and oh, so laudatory. Bless my precocious little heart, but the adults did like me. They could count on me to be bright, poised, and polite. They patted my head, paid serious court, and called me beautiful. Naturally I basked in their adoring company and far preferred it to that of my peers.

My contemporaries made me shy and ill-at-ease. Easy repartee with boys and girls my own age came hard, especially as the teen years approached. The carefree, laughing girls who attracted the big men on campus made me seem pale in comparison. But now I am jumping way ahead to the turbulent teens, years beyond my little girlhood.

Sarah and I played together, fought each other, closed ranks, and became best friends. She was a delicate petite blonde, witty and popular, a terrific dancer from her earliest days. She collected friends, boys and girls, and I envied the way she moved, unaffected by shyness among her peers.

Despite my social discomforts, I loved school, craved the challenges, and cringed over mistakes. Errors haunted me, they were weaknesses I replayed time and again in my memory, accompanied by "if onlys." I had to be tops—*perfectly* tops, if possible.

Even a cursory glance at the literature on anorexia nervosa shows my feelings about school to be classic symptoms. The anorexic girl usually is a top student, accepting only perfection from herself. Many anorexics, although they show high intelligence, remain at a concrete level of conceptualization, a characteristic of young children. A rigidly high, self-imposed drive to meet ever-demanding expectations is a hallmark of anorexia nervosa. These girls are so devoid of feelings of self-worth that only perfection makes them feel acceptable and lovable by others.

My parents used to urge me to back off and relax. "Settle for C's," my mother advised, and I was furious at the suggestion. No one set such unreachable goals for me but myself. Where did the motivation come from? Perhaps I observed my parents demanding much of themselves and internalized that value. Many times I have speculated over the different turn I might have taken if my parents had demanded perfection of me. What sort of rebellion would I have staged then?

Missing school was anathema. One morning in first grade I overslept. My parents knew I needed the sleep so they did not awaken me, but what a royal fit I threw when I awoke and found I was not where I should be. The same driving tenacity forced me to attend school even with the Asian flu of 1957. My goal was never to miss a day in four years of high school, and I did not.

As a student I was fiercely competitive. To meet the demands I imposed on myself, I created handy little rituals. Shoes had to be set just so before bedtime, closet doors were left exactly the same each night. I had other prescribed things to say or do. These did not interfere really with anyone else, but they did establish certain parameters of my own behavior. They set the stage well for my later dietary and exercise compulsions, although most likely they were not the cause, but instead just early symptoms. Many anorexics follow similar patterns of superstitious behavior, as discussed in the last section of this book.

Early on I became caught up in causes. American Indians were the first. By the age of eight I had devised a language, donned a headband, and bribed my gentler sister into playing Indians rather than her more conventional games. I was a fervent supporter of the Indian way of life and always cheered the Red Man in the Saturday matinee cowboy and Indian duels. When as an adult I researched the subject of anorexia, I found to my amazement that even this fascination with cowboys and Indians is typical. I expect that even in childhood the future anorexic views the world in black and white. There are "good" and "bad" forces contending. I was fascinated with the Indians' stoic behavior and ability to bear pain, qualities I considered admirable. Perhaps that was part of my insistence on this steadfast loyalty.

Ours was a church-going family, involved with the community. My parents made church the focal point of Sundays, and I remember fondly the small town fellowship after services, the roast beef dinners browning in the oven, awaiting our return. I never yielded to any force which prevented my going to Sunday School, attending it as compulsively as I attended school. Only four Sundays in nine years did I ever miss; two with measles and two with mumps. On vacations or through blizzards, somehow my will persevered and my parents got me to Sunday School. But even then I knew that religious fervor was not dictating my attendance. Rather, by following rituals I was staving off misfortune and change. But extreme behavior often corrects itself with extremes in later years, and eventually I went through periods when I never attended church. I am still rebelling against what I perceive as the God Who failed.

Winters meant school, holidays traditions, and after school, radio programs. Depending on the day, I listened to "Sgt. Preston of the Yukon" or "Sky-King" or "The Green Hornet." I suffered those days when I could not get home from school in time to eat my peanut butter sandwich and listen to the exploits of my heroes, where simple good always conquered obvious evil.

Summers then and now were treasured times. Sarah and I walked many a droning summer afternoon to the library to check out the maximum number of books, which we always exchanged, thus doubling our reading. On Saturday nights we followed band concerts in the town square by games of tag, while the adults visited. Stores stayed open until 11:00 p.m. and there was an unhurried air of good will and conviviality.

And how I loved the summer trips to the farm with my father. There were alfalfa fields to race across and hay wagons to ride on. Those sights and sounds today evoke a nostalgia that almost hurts.

Summers were also guarded times because of the specter of polio, a disease my father feared above all for his little girls. We never swam in public pools or ate refreshments at movies while this scourge raged. What I most hated were the daily naps, but they were unavoidable. I felt demeaned by being too old for that "baby stuff." When the first vaccine was available, Sarah and I were in the group that received the initial batch in our town.

Adults did not get sick in my family or if they did, recovery was predicated on being up and about immediately. We children were monitored when we fell sick and the doctor was called to the house immediately, but adults did not give in to the weakness of being ill. I observed closely and internalized this value.

Cicadas make the loneliest sound in the world with their late summer dirges, even more so since one summer taught me to associate them with illness. That summer I had become sick and had to be in bed on an early evening. The cicadas seemed to sing a song of such loneliness that I wept for them and for me, whose body somehow had betrayed me by being sick. Everyone else was outside, wrapped in the cocoon of early twilight—everyone but me, with this weak, disgusting body.

In a twinkling my teen years arrived. I still related to middle-aged adults, wrote poetry and celebrated causes, and I still found my fellow adolescents intimidating. They seemed so at ease, the girls who flirted and who were pursued.

Never mind that adults, including strangers, said that I was beautiful. What could they know if the final arbiters of appearance, one's own peers, did not agree? Only years later was I to learn that my shyness meant aloofness to my classmates. They weren't judging my beauty at all. Our family was a comfortable haven, I was considered "a brain," and certainly I was reserved in my behavior toward my agemates. Ironically, I was intimidating them, and all the while I felt that they were leaving me out.

By and large I grew up peacefully, although not without some stresses. There were moments when I disliked the compulsion to be a model of decorum, moments when I yearned to be freed from the restraints of being a "lady." Yet simultaneously, above all, I craved the approval of the adults around me. I was a fierce competitor for top grades, and yet I cringed when I heard cries of "teacher's pet." Opposing forces were at war within me more than I realized at the time.

The more I strove to be the best, the greater was the next challenge. By the time I was a junior in high school, there seemed to be a tacit agreement on the part of those who knew me that somehow I would do Great Things, whatever those might be.

But the greater share of pressure emanated from within me. Mistakes were anathema to me, assiduously to be avoided. After all these years, one of the most potent memories of grade school is the day I misspelled the word *birthday*.

As high school days came along, the need to be perfect still plagued me. Many of my friends took drivers' education and received their licenses upon turning sixteen. I did not take the course at school, but enlisted my father as my instructor. Anxious not to fall behind my classmates in anything, I took the test anyway after only a few lessons. My father advised me to wait because I was not ready. Of course he was right.

I did fine on the written part of the exam, but my performance behind the wheel didn't pass the test. As I was leaving the test area, a friend chanced by and inquired how I had done. The urge to be a regular kid overcame all else and I lied that I had passed.

Late that evening my parents somehow learned—probably I admitted—what I had done. They were appalled at the out-and-out lie, and the episode turned out to be one of the few tearfully stormy scenes of my youth. I never made them see how important it was to me to be like all the others, even in this one area. To them, a lie was a lie. My argument was specious. Just two weeks later I passed the test legitimately but it wasn't as satisfying as I had hoped. The early luster of success was dimmed by the lie and the scene it caused.

During that small town era, girls had to protect their reputations, in theory if not in fact. All of us nurtured the illusions of sobriety and virginity, even when we might have acted otherwise.

Plenty of girls "went all the way," of course, but no one let it be known. Officially, it was not the thing to do.

In the midst of these moral ambiguities, my nickname was the Ice Princess. If it denoted strict self-control and upright behavior, I earned the sobriquet. I lived up to my mother's succinct advice: "Girls, keep your skirts down and the boys will keep their pants up."

I was incredibly naïve and unprepared to cope with an attraction to boys. The openness about sexuality that exists today was unheard of then, and drugs were some peculiar phenomenon of the ghetto in faraway Eastern cities. The cigarettes and alcohol that some of my peers surreptitiously indulged in did not appeal to me; I was not about to tarnish my image. I now know, through study as well as reflection, that issues of sexuality are crucial in understanding anorexia nervosa. Many researchers believe that the anorexic girl uses the illness to delay or stop menses, unwilling to cope with the challenge of her emerging womanhood. She is seeking to stay in every way a little girl, for whom there are fewer threats and more protection. The incipient anorexic often entertains distorted notions about boys, sex, and pregnancy. Goodness knows, I had my own odd ideas.

The first I remember, from when I was eight, and my older sister became pregnant. I was elated at the prospect of a baby in the family, but I also remember worrying that somehow I might become pregnant too. I realized that being married seemed to be essential for pregnancy (little did I know), but I had no idea of the mechanics involved. Despite curiosity, I never asked.

Later a second misconception surfaced, this one less explicable. At 12 years old I harbored the disquieting fear that dancing too close to boys might also induce a pregnancy. The sad thing is that I was old enough to go to boy-girl parties, and still I remained so misinformed. By then I vaguely knew something of the process, but I must have sublimated the knowledge and the curiosity for more, to the extent that I could distort it in that way.

Public speaking was an outlet custom-designed for me, or so it seemed. It gave me an audience and capitalized on my talent at molding words around thoughts. This combination captured my interest and I made over fifty speeches in my junior and senior years. The resulting accolades were music to my ears and I *knew* that wonderful things, undefined as yet, were awaiting me.

Outstanding student, English award, National Honor Society, American Legion Oratory Award—senior honor day was mine. Two B's marred my 4.0 grade average, but college lay ahead, another chance to win that "perfect figure."

The summer between high school and college found me occasionally dating a man of 28. He charmed me, attracted me, and awakened my slumbering sexual urges. I was flattered by the attention of a *man*. I believe I was equally attractive to him, and physical involvement was a real possibility. Yet blithely I assumed that because of his age he would make no demands that I could not meet. Only now, looking back, do I realize the burden I placed on him. But nothing happened to mar my unassuming innocence. I think he realized more than I that a platonic relationship could not continue. He stopped calling.

Once during that summer I tried on a bathing suit and felt disgusted with my image. My body was heavier than I wanted it to be, soft and white instead of firm, lithe, and brown. My appetite made diets last only a day or two, and I stayed as I was. No, I wasn't fat, but I wasn't fashion-model thin either.

Despite that feeling of dissatisfaction, that summer was a lovely hiatus season bridging the world of childhood and adolescence to the life of an adult coed. True, my five-year dream of studying medicine had to be sacrificed on the harsh altar of reality. My desire and talents finally had to confront truth on that particular goal, but I believed that somewhere out there lay the opportunity to make my imprint.

I began college on scholarship at a two-year school within commuting distance of home. The dean tossed down the gauntlet of challenge the day I registered, by remarking that a girl from my home town had been valedictorian several years ago. I inferred that he did not expect history to repeat itself. Then and there I resolved to graduate number one.

From the first day I loved everything about college. The quality of instruction was excellent and I liked the classroom demands.

Miraculously the popularity and peer acceptance that had eluded me in high school now came easily, in measure beyond my expectations or dreams. There was almost no campus activity in which I did not participate, no opportunity for dating lost. It was all totally gratifying, all great fun. My rather foreign appearance and classroom studiousness, both suspect in high school, brought admiration and compliments in college. If ever there was a time for me to build a self-concept, this was it.

Those fall days in 1960 remain even now a shining, unblemished time. Although I was too young to vote, I campaigned fervently for Jack Kennedy. He represented our youthful idealism and aspirations as no one else could have. Election night brought victory to much that I held dear. Life was so good.

But the main thrust of my college years was academic excellence, and toward that end I worked hard. I fretted over compositions and worked vainly for the professor's rare stamp of approval. For the first time I was exposed to the cutting edge of a stern perfectionist, and my essays came back nicked and scraped frequently. How discomforting to discover how much work my writing needed. Later I would call that once threatening teacher one of the finest I ever knew, but then his scathing criticism devastated me. Anorexics are notorious for being unable to accept criticism. They won't argue with the source. They bury their responses, agonize over the criticism, and fervently resolve to do better.

It happened that in modern European history class there was a university transfer student named Joe Heater. He was currently dating my good friend, although they were not serious. Joe and I began to study together occasionally and then began to date. Numerous obstacles arose to keep us from developing a serious relationship, but they could not prevent its happening.

So many years later it is difficult to remember the igniting sparks. We have grown and changed too much. Perhaps it was Joe's unhesitant grasp for the brass ring, his self-assurance and take-command qualities that attracted me. He seemed to know where he was going and how to get there. As single-minded and goal-oriented as I was, I began to see life with this young man as more important than a doctorate degree, than the great American novel, or even than that most demanding taxmaster, unqualified adult approval. Besides, there was another girl for whom he had mixed feelings. This fact honed my competitive sword and I became determined to win this boy, partly spoken for, as mine.

Of course we differed greatly about the terms of our relationship. The old double standard was still prevalent in the early 1960s. The boy had nothing to lose and the girl apparently everything, or so generations of us had been told and believed. It was a deeply etched code indeed.

The conflict created a genuine moral dilemma for me. Desire contended on one side against all the dictates of my rearing on the other. I had to see the issue in black and white, with no compromising grays. Inexperience left me unaware that self-control could become exceedingly difficult. And yet I wanted to please Joe too, somehow *earning* his affection and esteem. I always felt that intense drive to satisfy every requirement in any situation.

We argued, fought, broke up, and came back together. Each time I was the loser, the one who felt defeated and victimized by the desires of my own body. Why should one's physical being get entangled in thoughts and feelings? It was a war of attrition, with so many intangibles at stake. Whichever way I went, I lost.

Either Joe was gone or else I gave in and sacrificed an engrained principle of my behavior. It was not sexuality that I wanted to repress but all the *conditions* that accompanied it. Surely reason should be able to overcome the demands of my body.

One must remember that twenty years ago, sexual mores were vastly different. Rarely has moral behavior changed as rapidly and drastically as it has since 1960. The Viet Nam War, campus unrest, the women's rights movement, and the heightened use of drugs have all played a role in the change, which occurred with disquieting speed. Women my age were caught on the very fringes, although most of us were still enmeshed in the standards of our mothers and grandmothers. Victorian morals ran a race against the moon rocket standards of the '60s and '70s. The times were out of sync and we, victims of time and place, suffered through with personal unrest and confusion.

Hail Mary, full of grace, the Lord is with thee:
Blessed art thou among women.
Blessed is the fruit of thy womb, Jesus.
Pray for us sinners now and at the hour of our death.

Chapter 2

Despite my superstitions, I had never believed in Friday the 13th, until that one Friday the 13th came along and marked a turning point in my life. Rather like the Two Roads in Robert Frost's poem, that night offered alternatives, but finally sent me down one route that changed my life.

From October to January I had played with fire in my relationship with Joe. The potential danger of increasing physical intimacy was always there, but I seemed to manage to remain oblivious to it. Chaste good night kisses became less and less satisfying to both of us. Longer kisses evolved into necking, necking evolved into petting, and. ... The foregone conclusion should have been obvious. It was to Joe, but not to me.

On that cold night, in the classic parked car, on Friday the 13th of January, we "went all the way," in the euphemism of the time. Even now the memory causes me to rationalize. It happened unexpectedly, without my consent. *It was a mistake*, but it couldn't be reversed. The irrevocable damage had been done. I was a scarlet woman—ruined and scared, simultaneously angry and relieved. It wasn't a peak experience for either of us.

Later that night, alone in my bedroom, I prayed desperately, first to be forgiven and second, not to be pregnant. I promised God that if He could somehow find forgiveness and protection possible, I would never do that again. Yet, amidst my fervent, abject prayers I felt bewildered. How could God have let me do such a thing? How my self-image now was tarnished. Yet, with the tiniest voice deep inside, a strangely exultant voice spoke through, saying that I was an adult now, a sexually experienced, loved woman! The forces were at war within me. But when forces go to war, one always loses.

The issue of repetition did not arise for some time. Joe left for the university 200 miles away. Oddly, he didn't tell me he was going. I found out only after the fact. I felt like I had been pushed off the high dive into an empty pool. Crash—shatter.

And yet we wrote each other, talked on the telephone, and proclaimed unwavering devotion. I believed that Joe really loved me. I *had* to believe it—I couldn't accept any other idea.

Summer vacation reunited us and the old pressures re-engaged. Once one tastes forbidden fruit, the appetite is whetted. Sex almost became a weapon. We both used it, but for different purposes. Joe traded me his love for physical gratification. I exchanged my favors to keep him from other girls.

The pattern seems unhealthy today, but it was typical behavior for the time. So many social strictures operated to make premarital sex wrong. And I well knew that I was risking valuable family disapproval, not to mention the possible heartbreak I might cause them. I believed that my actions were so bad that my parents could not possibly live with the reality. Now, looking back, I see that attitude as injustice on my part.

Somehow protection and passion did not mesh. To consider mechanical precautions indicated premeditation. As in murder, that only makes the crime worse. Consumed with worry on one hand, I went blithely ahead on the other, denying the reality of the situation.

Inevitably our luck ran out. Oh my God, what to do? I lived through those desperate days with a sense of detachment, as if I were looking down, an impartial observer, watching the frantic little ant scurry for cover. The ultimate horror had occurred, but somehow I remained calm, always preferring to worry about it tomorrow.

Except that I was sick, miserably nauseated, almost from the first. There I was, active in school, rehearsing for a play, being Little Miss Outstanding. Vomiting was out of the question. I willed myself not to throw up. To this day I can look at a chocolate pinwheel cookie and feel sick.

Joe had heard that quinine could induce a menstrual period. So I took quinine. Vile tasting stuff. All it did was make me dizzy and sick. So much for Old Wives' Tales.

How long I would have gone without taking action I really don't know. I was inertia personified. By not acknowledging the reality, I kept hoping that it did not exist. Even after I went to an out-of-town doctor and came back with a positive rabbit test, still I insisted on denial. Such naiveté.

Then one somber February afternoon my mother gently took me in her arms as if I had scraped my knee and said, "Sandra, you're pregnant." That audacious world kept right on rotating. Only vague recollections remain. I did realize that the only possible solution was marriage, as hastily as possible. And yet in the back of my mind lurked another alternative. The image of a final swim in an icy lake flitted in and out of my mind. But a germinal idea crept in and ever more tenaciously implanted itself. There was another alternative. Perhaps I could have my cake and eat it too. There was a way out, short of marriage or self-destruction. The notion was so horrendous, however, that I kept it buried deep inside.

After my mother brought the truth into the open, days went by quickly, all in a blur. Somehow I found myself in company with my mother and Sarah on the way to the doctor who had conducted the rabbit test. He was, conveniently, *not* the family doctor. I remember I rode the thirty miles to his office hunkered over. Now I wonder if my memory is symbolic, if maybe it did not happen that way at all. I can clearly remember, however, my younger sister's tearful outburst, the meat of which was deep disappointment in the sister she idolized. How could I have done this? What would people say? That memory pains me, but at least it was honest emotion, openly expressed. It was also absolutely the only time she ever mentioned the subject. Period. Silence.

Later that grim day Louise, my older sister, hugged me and asked if I were okay. I can't remember my parents saying very much to me, and to this day I can only imagine the feelings they had. My family protected me by silence, by carrying out a quick but well planned wedding, and by doing what one must—our motto, I think. Would it have made a difference later if we had raged a bit at each other, shouted out the pain, and then worked to heal the wounds? How do you defend yourself against infinite kindness?

Nor did my future parents-in-law ever say a word. They and I had established a genuine trust and affection, which I ached to see jeopardized. To my knowledge, that remained intact as long as they lived.

Either Joe and I felt we were in love, or we convinced ourselves that we were. I hadn't the strength to hold out against the assembled forces urging us to the altar, nor in many ways did I want to. Half of me wanted to be married to the boy I adored. The wishes of the other half, which yearned to remain free to grow and explore, remained unanswered.

Before the point of not return I voiced my hidden solution. I told Joe that I would have an abortion. At first he was astonished by the idea, but he quickly saw it as a solution. I trusted him, relied on him, to find out who could help me out. In 1962 a woman had to seek out a clandestine practitioner. There were no legalized abortions available then. And let me tell the anti-abortion forces one thing. If a woman wants an abortion, she will find a way.

It felt like a grade B movie. The winter was unusually harsh that year, even for the Midwest. The sun rarely shone. One bitter Saturday, sleet driving down, Joe delivered me to a drug store in a run-down part of the city. With shaking legs I sneaked in a back door and up a dark flight of stairs. Part of me felt dissociated from my body. I was participant and observer at the same time. It couldn't be real—and yet it was.

A tiny, timid tap on an unmarked door was answered by the sleaziest redhead I had ever seen. Even then the situation struck me as a caricature, a gross distortion of reality. She had to be late middle-aged, with flamboyantly dyed hair and a slip hanging below a henna-colored dress that warred with her hair.

"Yeah?"

"I, uh, understand you help girls like me." What if I'm wrong? You can't just ask someone for an abortion.

"That depends. How old are you?"

"Almost twenty."

"Sorry. Ya gotta be twenty-one in this state." She started to close the door.

"Wait, please. Isn't there something you can do?" *Am I really pleading with this ugly ogre?*

"Are you married? If you are, then it's okay. Yeah, all you need's a husband and $150." She might have been selling day-old bread for all the feeling she displayed.

Married as a condition. That sealed it. "I'm getting married, next Friday in fact."

"Okay, kid. Come in and I'll tell you what to do."

The place may not have been as dirty and cavernous as it appeared, but I think it really was. It reeked of a stale medicinal odor. Cobwebs hung all over. So much for concern with antiseptic conditions.

"Who are you anyway?" she asked me. I would have lied but by then she had told me I needed proof of marriage and I knew she would spot the discrepancy. For years afterward I feared that she kept organized records on all of her "patients." Much later, common sense made me realize that we would protect each other's identity in this ugly business.

She scribbled down some instructions on a prescription pad and told me to come back at 8:00 a.m. the morning after the wedding.

"Oh, hey, tell that guy of yours: no sex. You're more likely to get infection. Anyway, he obviously isn't a frustrated bridegroom." She cackled in a way that raised goosebumps.

Could I do it? There was still time to back out. And if I did, what then? School would end for both of us and we would become mired in early marriage, early baby, hopelessness forever. Besides, my reputation would be shot!

If anyone could see the tumult, the emotional war inside me, nothing was said. Showers and a bridal luncheon were hastily arranged. We were playing out our roles with full panoply.

The morning after our formal church wedding, complete with a smiling bride in gown and veil delivered from her father's arm to a waiting groom, I appeared at the appointed place and hour. My thoughts were still in neutral. Carefully I stayed on remote control. Panic wouldn't do. I could let myself die a little inside, but I couldn't let the façade crack.

My red-haired deliverer explained that her assistant was sick and I would have to come back on Wednesday. Stay of execution, prolonged agony.

Tuesday night Joe and I talked hard and late. He insisted that only I could make the decision. I knew what he *wanted* me to do; it just seemed so much less complicated to fall in obediently. Joe was fast becoming the significant force, the one to whom I turned for crucial guidance.

Wednesday morning: go to school, attend play practice, and then...Wednesday afternoon, 2:00 p.m.: old-fashioned black leather couch, harsh, cold instruments, bare hands, excruciating cramps, moments, a lifetime, a death begun. Her part was over. The abortive process was begun. One more girl helped out of a jam.

As she had instructed, I met Joe afterwards at a park, to jump and run in a travesty of early springtime renaissance. It was supposed to expedite the abortion. It seemed peculiar that the day should be unusually warm and sunny, an ironic backdrop for destruction.

Late in the afternoon Joe dropped me at the apartment of the assistant, a coarse-voiced broad who looked tough but somehow likeable, with her wry, worldly-wise attitude. She had seen a lot of us come and go. I couldn't eat, she said, because of complicating nausea. That was okay because I wasn't very hungry. We watched television a while. I distinctly remember: it was *My Three Sons*. In a way it was almost a congenial evening between friends.

About 3:00 a.m. the predicted cramping began. It was uncomfortable, but not as painful as it had been that afternoon nor as painful as I later knew real labor to be. Before dawn the assistant accompanied me to the bathroom. Into a red Folger's coffee can I delivered a male fetus. I wouldn't have realized gender but she was eager to show me. I was fascinated at how many recognizable baby features the fetus already had. The woman assured me that she would "toss it out later."

A pill swallowed, I slept several hours. About noon—a lifetime later—she prepared a chicken dinner and ordered me to eat. I ate. To this day I can see that pink bedroom/sitting room as if I had been there yesterday. On the wall was the prayer of Alcoholics Anonymous. I have waited twenty years for "serenity to accept what I cannot change."

Yo soy Yo.
—The Spanish affirmation *I am I*

Chapter 3

I was happy to be Joe's wife, yes, but I was also shaken. I had veered from my course. Later in the spring I was chosen track queen and it felt very funny to be written up as Mrs. Joe Heater. My own identity as Sandra Harvey was still emerging, too fragile yet to meld harmoniously with another.

The battle for top rank at school raged between an older man from Germany and me. Determination carried the day and I ranked first. It was a sweet victory, one to toss into the teeth of those who had opposed my marriage.

That summer went by in a blur of classes and work for Joe and a job for me that I detested. We moved in with his parents for two months and rarely saw each other. I felt estranged from my family and home, the place I had lived until the day of my wedding. The separation occurred unnecessarily, out of youthful pride and misinterpretation. Joe decided that he had lost my family's approbation by interfering with the brilliant future that I had supposedly tossed aside to marry him. Later the in-law relationship would deepen into one of mutual respect, harmony, and love. But in those early months we were too preoccupied to read the signals correctly.

Somehow there lurked inside me the notion that I, the golden girl, had disappointed those who had always been eager to see me soar. Being married suggested an end to career aspirations, a cop-out, a choice of heart over head. The year was 1962, and conditions were different for women. There was less acceptance of women who were full-time professionals, as well as being wives and mothers. We were still operating under an either/or system. As an example, I had been receiving a generous scholarship from a national women's organization. But when I got married, the scholarship was revoked automatically. They did not "waste" their money on married women.

There was never a question in our minds that Joe and I would finish undergraduate school. He had a football scholarship, I an academic one. We did not expect the next few years to be easy but we were willing to sacrifice things in the present for a brighter future. I was determined to be a top student at my transfer college, partly to prove wrong those who saw my marriage as a handicap. I had finished junior college with this impetus; my next step must conform to the same plan.

Despite our poverty-level income, those were happy days. It was surprising how often one or the other of our parents had an extra package of T-bones or too much laundry soap. We scrimped, of course, but we never felt deprived. One of our self-indulgences was frozen pecan pie. When the budget permitted, we bought one and then proceeded to husband it out wedge by wedge. Somehow it doesn't taste as good today, when we can afford pecan pie more frequently.

The Pill was still unproven in the early 1960s, and nobody we knew used it. Thus it was that I became pregnant in December, a condition shared at one time or another by virtually all of us in married student housing. It would seem that after the price exacted we would have wanted to buy more time. The cost had been high enough. But now it was *acceptable* to be pregnant. We had been married long enough!

Severe nausea was an early consequence of my pregnancy, and I nearly became dehydrated. Those first weeks were miserable and classes became a hazy blur to endure. Nevertheless I was determined not to let my grades suffer. Wasn't there still something to prove? At least this time I could vomit overtly.

My obstetrician was the same one who had delivered my younger sister and my nephew, crossing a span of several years. The women in the family considered him the best and I chose him on that reputation. In this area I would not compromise. Had I been Rh-negative I would have told the doctor that this was my second pregnancy. No other baby would be jeopardized, ever. But the problem didn't arise. In fact, when the doctor talked to Joe and me together I was so glib with answers that later Joe complimented me for my poise. Had he expected me to gush forth my secret to the obstetrician?

Dr. W. was strongly opposed to weight gain. He allowed his mothers ten to twelve pounds only and chided—not gently—if one exceeded her quota for the week or month. Even after the nausea left and my appetite returned, I monitored myself carefully. It became a point of pride to stay under the allotted gain. Recent research shows that insufficient weight gain can be harmful during pregnancy, but it seemed a good idea at that time.

I took summer school classes in order to have a lighter first semester with a baby due September 6. As it turned out, July 24, a week before summer school ended, I fell very hard. Two days later our first daughter was born, premature, tiny, and with hyaline membrane. Reassurances to the contrary, I blamed my clumsy self for Traci's premature birth. Obedient all along, I had actually lost body weight throughout my pregnancy. What a good girl was I! A kind of poetic justice was served, for as I lay in that hospital bed waiting for my precious daughter to live or die, I had a crucifix to stare at on, yes, a pink wall. St. Joseph's Hospital had within its wimpled sisters' midst a first class sinner: me.

Despite my concerned agony, I was convinced that God would not let Traci die. My reasoning was that I deserved to be punished most severely but God, being a New Testament God of mercy, would not wreak his vengeance this way. Oddly distorted comfort. Traci lived and thrived and I waited still for retribution.

The final year of undergraduate school was a whirlwind. Joe and I staggered schedules so that one was with Traci and the other was in class. The hardest part occurred during Joe's student teaching days when he lived forty miles away and I had to juggle the baby and classes. But we managed, and I graduated with highest honors, one of the top students in my class.

Graduation, moving, a summer job for Joe, a teaching contract occupied our time that summer of 1964. We rented a small cottage on the grounds across from my parents. Soon basic differences in upbringing and priorities arose. Joe's mother had always worked outside the home. She loved people and selling; she delighted in her job. On the other hand, my mother had been the complete homemaker and civic person. While Joe expected me to work, I believed my first responsibility was toward Traci's care.

I couldn't please everybody. One or the other, husband or child, would be shortchanged.

During the summer that we lived across the street from my parents, they extended an open invitation to Traci and me for lunch. This chance for family companionship, for a return home, meant so much to me. But Joe bristled, saying that he could provide for us. He forbade me to go. Whom to hurt? We were young and stiff-necked in those days, novices in communication. I accepted his edict, but inwardly I seethed.

August found us moving to Council Bluffs, Iowa, where Joe would teach and coach. With my bachelor of arts degree I was certified to teach only under special circumstances. I wanted to do my part, but I still felt a strong pull to be a full-time mother.

In October another inadvertent pregnancy resolved that question for awhile. We both felt resentful. Once again it seemed that my undisciplined body had succumbed to impulse and had betrayed me anew. Ultimately there should be some sort of punishment for such weakness. Shouldn't there?

This time I felt no nausea or discomfort. We were too far away to see Dr. W. regularly, so I selected a physician nearby. He was much less concerned about a limited weight gain, but I decided to follow the guidelines of my earlier doctor. The new doctor was involved in counseling as a corollary to his practice. He was the sort of person one confides in easily. During the course of his routine questioning I began to divulge my secret. More and more pent-up emotions tumbled out and I experienced a cathartic relief. He spent several hours listening non-judgmentally. I was late getting home, which angered Joe. He was livid when I told him why. Tentative overtures to openness, even with a professional, received negative reinforcement. Stiff upper lip, girl. Keep those feelings *in*. I watched my weight very carefully once again and delivered my second baby at a net loss. Joe was proud of my efforts, happy that my shape stayed reasonable.

Kim, our second daughter, missed arriving on Father's Day by only a few hours. Immediately she began to establish herself as an infant force to be reckoned with.

From her earliest moments she did not appear to find infancy the desirable human condition. She slept very little and she wanted only me to care for her. Shortly after her birth we moved from an upstairs to a basement apartment. Two little girls filled my days. Busy days, yes, but frustrating also to one who is not basically domestic. I constantly felt tired, up three or four times a night with Kim, and I felt a constant nagging guilt that by staying home I was being unfair to Joe.

Each evening I deliberately let the apartment become messy in order to have something to do the next day. Of course I read to the girls and played with them. We took walks every nice afternoon. But I felt isolated. It was hard to force myself into the mold of a creative homemaker. I simply did not fit. Yet this was the role I had chosen and defended.

Deep down a nagging sense of failure tugged at me over the next three or four years. Joe had his teaching, coaching, and evening graduate classes. By then I had two daughters, a basement apartment, and an occasional short-term teaching job.

How well I recall my feeling of frustration and defeat on my twenty-fifth birthday. A quarter century had passed and there was nothing of *significance* to show—no doctorate earned, no novel written, nothing, really, in my judgment. I had failed to live up to my early promise; I must be as disappointing to others as I was to myself.

Were these thoughts the seeds that bloomed into thistles of self-destruction? If I could not control my own destiny, might I not at least control my own body?

Still these were not totally unhappy times. Most evenings after the girls were in bed Joe and I would read or watch television, companionably sharing pizza or potato chips and Pepsi. In fact, my addiction to Pepsi was a family joke. We always kept them and I would drink two a day.

Kim walked at an early age; both girls learned to talk early, which made them fun. I doted on my daughters with every fiber of my being, but I still felt guilty not earning part of our income.

Slowly but surely opportunities came. Correspondence courses provided my teacher-certification credits and I started to teach in an adult education program at night. Then came summer school teaching and gradually I began to earn money to help fill the family kitty.

At about this time I became a devoted fan of exercise expert Jack LaLanne, who then appeared daily on television. I would don leotard and shorts and agonize through the contortions he demonstrated. I also decided at about this time to lose a few pounds by eating mostly oranges. This diet lasted all of two days. Joe and treated it as a joke. We also laughed because during Jack LaLanne commercials I would dash to the kitchen to nibble coffee cake or peanut butter.

We were far enough ahead early in 1967 to start looking for a house to buy. Then women's incomes were rarely considered, so we had to assure the lending officer that I did not intend to become pregnant again.

The ideal house turned up, a two-story Cape Cod on a shady corner lot. The house was red with white shutters. The yard was surrounded by a charming rail fence. Our parents each loaned us half the down payment, which we proudly and gratefully returned six weeks later, once I had received my summer school check.

As the June sun streamed through the windows on the Sunday we moved in, I truly believed that this was our happily-ever-after house where we would grow together as a family. Years later when we lived in a house three times as large and the little girls had become young women, I pondered over how much of ourselves we had left behind, and at what price.

Days filled up with more home and teaching duties. Now I was earning regularly too, so I felt more at ease. Traci and Kim were all any mother could want. They were healthy and bright, ever fascinating to their parents.

But still some hard inner dictator kept reminding me that all of this was still not enough. A diary entry for Jan. 13, 1968, expresses it thus: "Every once in a while one is confronted with pure, cold reality and realizes there will never be an earthshaking contribution from oneself, not even a tiny tremor! It's hard to 'front life' and look to the basic facts. At 25 *This Is It.* If I were sure I am doing well what I am doing, that would be some compensation."

I could find no way to dispel the feeling that I had once had the promise but was not meeting the burden of delivery. It was just a matter of time before I would retreat into the deepest recesses of myself in an effort to establish dominance once more. I *would* control my destiny and accomplish some great feat if it cost me my life to do it.

We look before and after,
And pine for what is not;
Our sincerest laughter
With some pain is fraught.
    —Percy Bysshe Shelley, 'To a Skylark'

PART 2
The Fall

The Fall

The descent began innocuously, on a crisp spring evening. The end of a beautiful, ordinary day. But before the drama played its final scene, I was to plunge into a maelstrom of self-destruction that threatened my life, my marriage, and the happiness of those I held most dear. This is the story of a journey into hell and back. Unfortunately it is not my experience alone but one that affects other victims in increasing numbers.

Saturday, May 24, 1969, was a bright day, sunny and cool. I remember working outside, mowing the yard and playing tag with Traci and Kim. They were five and three years old. Joe worked alongside, completing the picture of a secure young American family. That evening we went to a small Omaha fish restaurant where I thoroughly enjoyed the house specialty, for which the restaurant is well known.

- En route home we decided to buy a few spring clothes. I tried on a pair of madras slacks. Lo and behold I took a size 14. I felt instant disgust with myself for getting flabby and out of shape, especially since I had just eaten a large, rich meal. Then and there I resolved to trim off and firm up my plump 27-year-old body.

As soon as we got home that evening I decided to start firming up immediately. Ten sit-ups and six leg raises were more than enough, but I felt reasonably self-righteous in having made a start.

Perhaps if results had come more slowly or had been less noticeable, I would have quit my diet in discouragement. After all, I had made half-hearted attempts for several years to lose ten pounds, only to give up within two or three days. This time, though, the pounds came off quickly. I commenced each day with fifteen minutes of calisthenics.

During those last days of May my husband was wrapping up his year as a public school teacher and coach. I was completing my own school year in a private pre-school and teaching night classes to adults. We were busy, and we seldom got together for meals.

Whatever the reasons, by Memorial Day I had lost six pounds. The size 14s in my closet were noticeably looser when I tried them on. This early success bolstered my efforts and helped alleviate the pangs of hunger, even fewer as the days went by.

I seemed to enjoy the discipline of self-denial. After all, failing at anything signified weakness, did it not? All my life I had wanted to succeed in attaining whatever goals I had set. Dieting would prove no exception.

When I had lost ten pounds, Joe suggested that I looked slim enough, even rather gaunt. I bristled at his criticism, aimed at my success, and continued on my losing ways.

One early June weekend my sister and brother-in-law came to visit. They immediately noticed my weight loss and commented that I had certainly taken off enough, having now lost twelve pounds. Their noticing just strengthened my resolve to lose a few more pounds. Each lost pound became a sort of triumph, proof that I was self-disciplined and strong enough to withstand temptation.

And thus began the ritual of weighing in. Never has a wrestler watched scales more assiduously. The appointment with my new god, the bathroom scale, came first every morning. It was with an accelerated heartbeat and sweaty palms that I approached the weigh-in altar. A pound lost was a triumph. A pound, or less, gained represented a moral defeat. Either result had the same effect: redoubled effort to watch the needle move ever downward.

Of course daily weigh-ins soon grew insufficient. Within three weeks the ritual was repeated more than once a day. Even an innocuous glass of water became an enemy, because it could ever so slightly tip those scales.

Meantime my exercise routine increased in duration and intensity. First there was a required fifteen-minute stint each day, but soon this lengthened to half an hour and then an hour. I augmented sit-ups and calisthenics with bicycle riding. All this from one who was not an athletic person!

Somewhere in my mind I set 110 pounds as my goal. I was

determined to reach it by June 18. Why that date? A childhood friend whom I had not seen in several years planned to visit my parents then. Joe, the girls, and I were going there for the weekend to see Susan and to celebrate Kim's fourth birthday. I intended to present them with my new slim self.

By now calorie counting had become an obsession. During one three-day period I consumed a total of 320 calories, while maintaining a busy schedule and exercising strenuously. Even those few calories I begrudged.

How was I able to diet this vigorously? Almost all occasional dieters give up fairly quickly out of physical weakness, disgust, boredom, or neglect. Most people experience real discomfort from serious dietary deprivation. Yet I almost never felt weakness, and never a headache or lightheadedness. Of course these symptoms, or lack of symptoms, are characteristic of the anorexic curse. Somehow the diet becomes all-filling, all-consuming. But then I knew nothing about anorexia nervosa.

Joe had a summer job with the railroad, I had one as a summer school teacher. So we found ourselves together for even fewer meals than we had shared in late May. The girls were too young to be aware of any disturbance in patterns, anyway. At all costs I avoided eating (or not eating) at the same time as Joe lest he insist that I consume an extra detested calorie. By now he was determinedly sure that I had lost more than enough weight.

At the same time I delighted in buying all sorts of tempting morsels, as if in resisting them I was winning a moral victory. I almost force-fed my little daughters the food I was denying myself. I took vicarious pleasure in watching others eat the caloric riches I would not.

By June 18 I had met my goal. The end result, however, was not quite the scenario I had designed in my imagination. Susan and my parents noticed the weight loss all right, but with disapprobation. Instead of the pleasing compliments I expected, I heard how wan and ill I looked. I attributed this attitude to jealousy, forgetting that a loving, supportive family rejoices in any member's success.

During that weekend visit at home, on Kim's birthday, I took my first fall off the diet wagon. All these years later I can re-member the self-contempt and frustration that accompanied that momentary act of weakness, as I considered it then.

Binges are part and parcel of anorexia, although I did not know so at the time. An anorexic's binge does not just mean over-eating until one feels too full. Rather it is a secret, frantic compul-sion to devour everything edible in sight. A binge means eating a half cake, a quart of ice cream, four or five sandwiches, entire packages of crackers, anything else available. The binger prowls the kitchen opening the fridge, cabinets, and drawers, all the while stuffing in the food. She is barely conscious of any food she is eating and no normal warning bell signals satiety. Unleashed flood waters of obsessive eating engulf the marauding anorexic.

Before we returned home that Sunday my parents took us out to a new buffet for dinner. Two conditions affected my behavior there. The first was physiological. After several weeks of severe nutritional and caloric deprivation my body surely needed to re-plenish itself. The second was more psychological. I realized that my diet was earning marks of disapproval and causing genuine concern among my family. I was still visible to them through my peculiar behavior and changing appearance.

So I gorged at the buffet, but immediately felt intense self-hatred and a desire to flagellate my body, whose appetite had be-trayed me and defeated my self-control.

But oh, how good all the forbidden food tasted, that tempting smorgasbord of breads and pastries and other delicacies. After an occasional cup of bouillon or four ounces of diet fruit juice, ordi-nary fare would have seemed like ambrosia.

Back home that evening I brought out Kim's birthday cake which I had baked and frozen earlier. Like a starving animal I wolfed down piece after piece. I felt simultaneously nauseated and compelled to continue. By this time I was totally repelled by my own voracious behavior, full of self-directed anger, even hatred. I interpreted this one day of weakness as a disaster and I resolved to begin the remedy immediately.

I got on my bike to ride off as many calories as possible. It was a second-hand pedal bike with unreliable brakes. In my over-excitement I pedalled straight for an accident that broke my tailbone, now prominent, since I had lost so much weight. Ouch —more frustration! I was barely able to hobble home, let alone accomplish my nightly exercises. Thus, what should have been a delightful weekend ended on the sourest of notes.

By now I had to admit that I was hooked on dieting and exercise. My world began to revolve totally around those two facets of my existence. Husband, children, life in general became secondary considerations. And yet somehow my work did not suffer. To the contrary, I could not sit still. To do so would burn fewer calories, so somehow despite the food deprivation, my energy level soared, at least in this early stage of my illness. The effect I felt must be akin to the adrenalin high that accompanies a "flight or fight" situation. Yet instead of a momentary upsurge, my condition stayed elevated, day in, day out.

So I cleaned, scrubbed, mowed, laundered, and taught my classes. These physical activities intruded more and more on my time as a wife and mother. Although I don't remember clearly, quite probably I was a short-tempered shrike with the little girls I treasured.

Meantime, my behavior baffled Joe. I was later to learn that he thought another man had come into my life or something comparably drastic. He was also angry at me, confused to see me grow thinner by the week, long past the point of being attractive.

He alternated between disgust and despair. He would insist that I eat more—and yet he had no real idea of how little I ate— but that only solidified my determination to adhere to my diet.

One day before his 3:00–11:00 shift at the railroad he demanded that I eat a peanut butter sandwich in his presence. The idea revolted me—both the act of eating and Joe's insistence on it. I could not bear to surrender any measure of sovereignty over my body. To do so under duress, especially to eat a calorie-laden peanut butter sandwich, was the worst possible indignity I could imagine. I ate it, after he left I retaliated by a marathon bike-riding and exercise binge.

We sustained an uneasy truce, punctuated by similar occasional skirmishes, and we even continued with earlier plans to take our first family vacation, a trip to Minnesota. We would leave after summer school ended and before the school year began. ,

Secretly the idea of the vacation filled me with a deep fear. For the life of me I could not decide how I could curtail my eating to the point of fasting, as I was doing now, nor did I see how to work in the daily hour of vigorous calisthenics I had worked up to. What I had enthusiastically anticipated just weeks before now loomed as a major worry and source of defeat. This vacation was a threat, an encroachment into my secret universe of dietary compulsions.

The world went on, although I fit in only peripherally. A colleague's daughter underwent critical kidney surgery after prolonged and ineffective treatment. Despite intense worry over her daughter, my friend was stunned to see me when I dropped by.

People who had known me for years often looked twice to ascertain that it was really I. Somehow the rapidity of the weight loss combined with other physical manifestations had a dramatic effect. As pleased as I was to have the weight loss noticed, I could not ignore that the response was not complimentary. Most frequently someone would ask whether I was ill or tell me how bad I looked.

But I reveled in looking gaunt and wasted. Each protruding bone symbolized some sort of perverse victory. Like a typical anorexic, my body image was totally distorted. Even emaciation did not appear thin to me. I wanted to lose even more.

Despite days of virtual fasting, I retained an appetite and savored even the notion of food. The richer and gooier the better, I thought, but only in my mind. How vividly I remember the night Neil Armstrong walked on the moon. Joe came home early to see the event on television. On this historic, exciting occasion I was too absorbed in *me* to tune in to the importance of what was happening. Joe had come home hungry and I prepared a snack for him. Even now I can replay the battle I waged within myself, trying not to yield to temptation and taste the French bread or ham salad. Once, twice, three times my hand let the forbidden food graze my lips. And each time I fought off the urge to eat. Mine was the greater victory that awesome night of scientific triumph.

My success at resisting food felt more personally meaningful than man's first walk on the moon.

Joe and I thrusted and parried our way through July. My teaching ended on July 25, the day before Traci's sixth birthday. We were having a children's party for Traci, taking a group of her friends to the park. All of the youngsters had been Montessori schoolmates and I knew the mothers of the children. As parents dropped their children off, each commented on how thin and sick I appeared. The reference to "sick" was not pleasing, but "thin" was music to my ears.

The birthday party was not an unmitigated success, because of tension between Joe and me. I was caught in the dilemma of how to eat as little as possible, and by now my disposition was affected by such extreme dieting. But we coped and as young as the children were, they appeared not to notice any adult hang-ups or tensions.

The family party was another story. My younger sister and her husband came Saturday evening, before the others arrived on Sunday. Sarah took one look at me and burst into tears, a more intense reaction than I had experienced yet from anyone else. Even her attempts to reason with me failed, despite our closeness. For dinner that evening I ate a cup of vegetable soup while the others tried to eat the food I had prepared. Joe was at work, so I did not have to "perform" for him by eating more than I wanted or felt I needed or deserved.

Early the next morning at my ritualistic weigh-in the scale showed a three-pound gain! Rationally I knew that one could not gain weight on a near-fast, but there was the evidence. My 100 pounds of Saturday had become 103 on Sunday and I was incensed, irrationally angry.

The other family members, my parents and my older sister and her family, arrived by mid-morning. Later, they said my appearance had hit them as hard as a harsh physical blow. They all thought that I had lost my mind along with all that weight.

We are a family that believes in doing the correct thing in a social situation and we carried on, determined to have a good time at Traci's party. Now, when I look back at the photos, I can see the strain on everyone's faces. I look like a refugee from a concentration camp. Now I recognize the cause of their alarm, but at the time I could not see myself with any accuracy. Yes, I would have admitted to being slimmer, but I didn't consider myself too thin.

Louise says two things stunned her that day. Of course one was the way I looked. The second was my welcoming remark: "I've gained three f-----g pounds overnight on one cup of soup!" Never before had any of the women in our family ever used that sort of language. To this day I am convinced that she remembers and shudders. It just wasn't like me.

I took the occasions of my daughters' birthdays to go off the wagon. I gorged again on Traci's birthday, just as I had on Kim's birthday five weeks earlier. And again I did so for two reasons. First, I was *hungry*, but second, I wanted to allay the fears of my family and convice them that what they considered my foolishness was over. But even as I ate, deep down I knew that I would starve myself again.

That night was the first time I ever used laxatives to purge myself of food I wished I had never eaten, another frequent trick of the anorexic trade. I took several tablets, and they produced the desired physical effect. When Joe realized what I had done, with frustration and fury he flushed the remaining laxative tablets down the toilet. He also questioned my sanity, speaking in tight-lipped, barely controlled anger. It was a miserable night, physically and emotionally.

Bedtime—usually the time for close communication between a married couple—turned into a verbal wartime instead. My body was wasted, I must have seemed totally repugnant as a sexual partner. Joe must have grown to hate the skeletal feel of my body, once curved and soft. Many a night, though, he held me like a hurt child and asked me, over and over, "Why?" Much later, after I had found myself again as a woman, Joe confessed, almost in shame, how he remembered the revulsion which kept him from making love with me. Every time he looked down, he said, he saw a snake instead of his wife. Even now the memory of that vision comes unbidden into my mind. I wonder whether it flits through his thoughts also.

The tragic thing is that I honestly did not know the answer to his constant question, "Why?" I could not answer his pleas, I knew no way to make him understand. At that time I could not explain the monkey riding my frail back. I still remember the stark horror of realizing something was woefully wrong with me and yet having no idea what or why. I had never heard of *anorexia nervosa* and had no inkling that anyone else suffered from this strange affliction. Looking back today, I am convinced that had any of us known or understood anorexia, I would have benefited immeasurably from the knowledge. Perhaps my story can help others who are today just as bewildered and alone as I was then.

It is ironic that I was so ignorant about anorexia because I delight in acquiring medical information. Studying medicine was my paramount goal for years and even after I gave up the professional goal, I gravitated toward medical journals and news. But somehow, even with all that reading, anorexia had never entered my vocabulary. The general population is still just as uninformed about this debilitating sickness as I was then. If recounting my personal pain makes even one victim or her family aware, then it has been well worth the effort.

Now I realize that, except for my age, I was an ideal candidate for this malady. Most victims are young girls, but I had just turned 27 at the onset of my illness, making me years older than the average victim. Still, all the other characteristics of anorexia were mine.

A typical profile anorexic is a young woman, a high achiever, usually very bright, self-disciplined, and regimented. She tends to be demanding of herself and prone to self-criticism. Often she has a high academic standing and lofty expectations.

Virtually every criterion applied to me. As a teenager I vowed that I would rather be dead than mediocre. Such ambition makes a relentless master. Anorexics always orient themselves toward a goal, and for me aspirations did not end with marriage and maternity. During all these years I had no hint as to what was coming; how blithely I danced through those dress rehearsals preceding anorexia. But I learned the hard way that one's world can become topsy turvy for no apparent reason. Only when one looks deeply will certain possible causes begin to emerge, and only then can one work through toward a cure. Early alertness to the characteristics of incipient anorexia can also help expedite the return to health.

But I didn't have the advantage of this wisdom during those first months of compulsive weight loss. Between 1964 and 1968 I had a variety of teaching assignments in summer school and adult education classes. I enjoyed it all but never felt a regular part of any system. In 1968 I received Montessori training and a handful of us worked hard to establish a school in Council Bluffs. We had to persuade people that the Montessori method works, build up an enrollment, work with parents, teach, and play the role of pioneers. It was rewarding, exhausting work. The part I liked best was selling the program, persuading the skeptical that Montessori properly used was beneficial to young children.

Montessori classes by day, adult education classes by night, my time was filled with satisfying work, through the spring of 1969.

The summer of '69 was typical for the Midwest; high heat and humidity, excellent conditions in which to dehydrate. The little food I ate was providing absolutely minimal amounts of liquid, and I disliked tea and coffee. Excessive exercise, inside and out-of-doors, forced me to drink something though. Besides, the constant, severe food deficit to which I subjected myself created a feeling of total emptiness. I refused to acknowledge weakness, but it became increasingly difficult to lift a child or push a vacuum. Finally I resorted to drinking lots of hot tea and, ultimately, coffee. Both beverages provided a caffeine kick for energy, and at least they imparted a momentary feeling of fullness. One grasps at straws to survive.

I began to experience the panic of brinkmanship and guilt. Gradually it came to me that I was flirting with disaster, that quite possibly my health was being irreparably damaged. Yet even this perception was insufficient to stop me. It was as if I were on the brink of destruction, but I was still willing to risk a fall over the edge. I felt two forces at war within me. One insisted that I had every right to control my own body. One's body, after all, should be one's private domain. But the other kept reminding me of reasons to feel guilty. I recognized the pain of my husband and family and regretted being the source of their discomfort, especially when such a natural, simple act as eating provided the solution. I had to connive and sneak to have my own way, which made it forcefully clear that my actions were amiss. I, who abhorred guile and subterfuge, had become a skillful sneak. It surprises me still to reflect on the ploys I used to keep from eating.

Deficiencies in essential vitamins and minerals threaten one's emotional well-being, and poor nutrition certainly did not help me clarify my thinking. It was as if a faceless, amorphous monster circumvented my every move. I awakened to a lowering cloud and carried it with me all day. Some nameless IT was in control of my life; a ferocious taskmaster, ever demanding more fasting and brisker exercise.

The more I lost control, the more determined I was to keep control. And still this vicious cycle had no identity to me. I had no clue that anyone else had *ever* endured this sort of hell.

The first week in August we went to visit both sets of parents for a few days before going to Minnesota. By now I was constantly cold from loss of body fat and food energy. I also experienced the corollary of malnutrition, the sickeningly sweet taste of ketosis. My body was using itself up, consuming its own muscle mass to get protein. My feet began to swell with the onset of pitting edema. As rapidly and as thoroughly as possible, I was becoming a victim of starvation in a nation of stocked supermarkets and a kitchen replete with food. At 5'4" and 103 pounds I resembled a skeleton. I already had lost 25 pounds.

We arrived at my parents toward midnight. It had been perhaps ten days since they had celebrated Traci's birthday with us. Both were stunned at how much worse I looked after that short time. I clung to my mother like a whimpering, scared child, heartbroken not to feel the joy of coming home anymore.

The next morning I went to the family doctor, a man who had known me for years. Dr. K's reputation was that of a fine medical doctor, cautious and thorough in diagnosis. I had known him for years and felt comfortable in going to him, indeed I *wanted* to go. Perhaps Dr. K. would name this strange malady and make it go away. His was a personal reaction of dismay as well as professional concern. He checked me and ordered extensive blood tests for the next morning. At least I had a legitimate excuse for fasting after 6:00 p.m. that night.

How I hate needles. I had always been in good health and had never had much experience with them. I had two other fears that morning: plain old childish cowardice and fear that the tests would reveal real damage. The situation did not improve a bit as the lab technician poked repeatedly to find my collapsed veins, another result of my starvation. Eventually she drew seven vials, in my opinion about all the blood I had left, and I went home to wait the required number of days for the results.

Amazingly, like most other anorexics, I experienced no lasting complications, and showed few physical effects, except for emaciation, even in the depths of my illness. Only at the point of nearly irreversible starvation would the lab findings be abnormal. My system showed no major damage—*yet.* The years of good health, my relative youth, and proper childhood nourishment stood me in good stead. You would think that now that I had lucked out, my common sense would assert itself. I would start eating, and our lives would straighten out. Or so you would think.

We decided not to take a vacation. Instead I would stay at my parents', visit Dr. K. each day, and subject myself to the temptation of my mother's irresistible cuisine. Joe and the girls went home, taking his parents with them to tend the children and help out.

For several days I went to the doctor regularly. He reminded me of my girlhood beauty, he tried hypnosis, he prescribed potent vitamins. I realize now that all he gave me were cosmetics put on over my own dirty face. Yes, he made sense, but I wasn't ready to work through and understand the problem. I would have to gain weight for my own sake, not to please anybody else, regardless of that person's importance in my life. And I did not want to gain!

I tried to cooperate during the two weeks I was my parents' little girl again. Reluctantly I ate small quantities of three meals a day. I took the vitamins. As nutrition assumed more normal levels my sense of well-being increased. It was as if my jangled, exposed nerve ends were being soothed and insulated once more.

I still struggled to retain rigid self-control, which I equated with denying myself food. Again I went through periods of gorging followed by deep disgust. By the time I went home in mid-August, my body had lost some of its waifish look, my sunken cheeks had a bit of fullness, but my attitude had not made the turn toward keeping me on the road toward normal health again.

Joe and I talked at length, trying to understand, to compromise. He saw 125 pounds as the goal. But I just wanted to clear out the cobwebs of my obsession. We agreed that 115 pounds would satisfy us both. It was a weight that was within easy reach physically, because I weighed 107 at this point. Neither of us knew then that months would intervene before I reached that magic number.

Off and on throughout the remainder of August and early September I struggled, resolving each day to try a bit harder, yet not really committed to gaining weight.

School resumed and I began evening teaching, along with my other teaching jobs. The children noticed how my appearance had changed. One little girl came up to tell me, with the clarity of a child's observation, that I had the skinniest legs she had ever seen. Other youngsters asked my daughter why her mother was so little, a difficult question for a four-year-old to answer.

Meantime Traci had started first grade. Sadly, I was dissipating my energies on myself almost exclusively, grappling with worries like: How can I avoid eating? Will I gain? Should I try to please Joe and my family, and gain? Or should I please me? And then there was the hour or more devoted to strenuous calisthenics, with which nothing must interfere. If one's mind is completely preoccupied with calorie counts, there is precious little left over to give to anyone or anything else.

Traci began first grade with great enthusiasm. But she soon found that she and her teacher were not on the same wavelength, and the year was miserable for my child. How I now regret the preoccupations that prevented my visiting school and working to alleviate the condition. Traci still shudders at the memory of first grade. It haunts me to remember how I tuned out at a critical time.

I continued the feast-or-famine mode of operation. On days that I feasted, generally weekends, I would accomplish almost nothing but eating. Momentarily the satiety was soothing, but the gorging soon led to feelings of self-loathing. One Saturday, for example, I had to bake cookies for the church coffee hour. Almost as fast as I baked, I ate.

It must be hard for one who has never binged to imagine the feeling. It is as if one is attacking an enemy in the form of food. I was able to consume prodigious portions, eating long past the point of fullness. I did not sit down at the table to eat, preferring to stuff myself in an almost uncivilized method. My attitude was "all or nothing." After days of eating 300 calories maximum, how hard it must be on one's system the next day to eat gluttonously. But I rationalized that if I had ruined a day by eating, then I might as well ruin it with gusto. All the time I was hating myself for lack of control. I was also building up hidden anger at Joe, for whom I was doing all this terrible gross overeating. As bad as they made me feel, now in retrospect, I believe that possibly those occasional binges gave me the nourishment to keep going.

We were living under a truce. We tried to avoid open warfare, but there were few moments of warmth. At night we went over and over the same catechism.

"Why are you doing this?"

"I don't know."

This opening litany led to more questions, but no real answers emerged.

Only one time, despite many moments of deepest despair, did I ever imagine myself dying. One hot evening, when I was forcing my exhausted body and swollen feet to continue biking, there came a fleeting notion that death would end all of this. Yet I never considered suicide. I had no intention of continuing this bizarre behavior to the point of irreparable harm—provided I could recognize that point, of course. Suicide among anorexics is extremely rare. Suicide is not the intent.

Finally Joe insisted that I see a psychiatrist. Our priest, who was also the Episcopal headmaster of the Montessori school, suggested someone whom he considered quite competent. But, in my mind, that was the ultimate degradation. My entire self-image was predicated on the idea of that I had utmost self-control, that I was rational and intelligent. I also prided myself on reticence where strangers were concerned. Consulting a psychiatrist represented to me a total break-down of my ability to cope. Still, I had to admit, deep within myself, that my current behavior was erratic. This obsession had become a cruel slave driver.

I phoned for an appointment and went first to talk with him on October 7. With the greatest trepidation I forced myself to check in and take a chair in the waiting room. Rather surreptitiously I glanced around to check out my fellow sufferers. With surprise I noticed that everyone in the waiting room looked calm and alert, as much as any group of people, except that they appeared unusually well-dressed and looked successful. My observation served to allay my fears about who consulted psychiatrists. They weren't either eccentric celebrities, one step removed from bedlam, or incompetents who could not function in the real world. Such stereotyping is unfortunate and costly to those who most need professional help.

Dr. J. proved to be very non-threatening. Instantly I felt some rapport with him. He was not judgmental, but he did not hesitate to offer comments. He sat across a desk from me and informed me that he was recording our conversation. There was no couch in sight, and another bit of stereotyping went down the drain.

At the end of the session the doctor remarked that apparently I had a sound perception of my problem. He prescribed tranquilizers to relax me. If I were not so tense and fearful perhaps I would find food less threatening. That was the explanation, but

I sensed that, at best, this was a Band-Aid solution. I accepted the prescription hesitantly. Taking tranquilizers also flew in the face of all my attitudes and feelings. They represented a crutch, a surrender to weakness, and I was determined never to take them.

In fact, I did take them, only for a few days. It felt like falling from a tall building and landing on my chin. I was wound up so tightly that the relaxing effect of the tranquilizer presented a painful contrast. They made me inordinately sleepy, to the point that I put my head on my desk and actually fell asleep in my classroom. I decided that tranquilizers were masking and muddling reality and that this was not the way to deal with the situation. Therefore, with great relief, I flushed the remainder down the toilet.

I shall never know whether tranquilizers would have benefited me. Perhaps I did not really give them a fair chance. I certainly should have discussed their disturbing effects with the doctor. But I have never been sorry that I did not become dependent on any medication. When the haze of anorexia finally ended, I could enjoy the sense of clarity free of any pills.

Ironically, the day before I went to see Dr. J. I had overeaten and then resorted to laxatives, a ploy that seemed grotesque even to me by that time. Such typical anorexic patterns should have shouted out the nature of my illness, but it took time before I could open up and talk about these habits freely with the doctor.

October went by without any noticeable improvement. My parents came to visit and again I made a big effort over food. Joe and I took them out to dinner Sunday and I forced myself to eat a big meal. All day I had overeaten, so I approached dinner physically sated. I had not taken a laxative, but later that evening I had diarrhea anyway. Mother had ordered the same item for dinner and she suffered from an upset stomach during the night, too. Joe, however, refused to believe my innocence. No wonder. He was convinced that I was still inducing my own illness. He was intensely angry and disappointed at yet another breach of trust, as he saw it. He ordered me to take the girls and go home with my parents until I came to my senses.

He wanted the girls with me for two reasons. First, his

coaching hours were long, making it difficult for him to care for two young children. The second reason I think was Joe's belief the girls' presence would remind me of my necessity as their mother. He reasoned that I would not just waste away with our little daughters to care for. I could focus on them instead of myself. I pleaded for one more chance, but my pleas availed not. Obediently and numbly I packed bags for the bewildered girls and me. The exile hurt a great deal. All my life I have wanted to be where I am supposed to be. My classroom was my responsibility. Traci was in public school and I did not want her to miss classes either, even though she was advanced in her studies and unhappy with her teacher anyway.

On a beautiful October Monday we left, to be gone for I knew not how long. We stayed ten days, as it turned out, and on most of those ten days I did put forth effort to gain weight. I weighed about 96 pounds when we went to my parents'. After ten days of concentrated eating, to near insensibility sometimes, I left on October 31 at least ten pounds heavier.

The girls and I took the train home that cold Saturday morning, against my parents' advice. They recognized that I had made progress, but they realized I was far from well. The very morning that we left, I refused more than a bite or two of breakfast, pleading possible train sickness. It was sickness all right, but not from a train.

As the train clicked over the tracks, taking me back to my regular life, I was torn. One part of me was pleased to present a heavier, more attractive woman to Joe, while the other side lamented the loss of total skinniness. This ambivalence had become intrinsic in my thinking.

Joe was so happy to have us back and was complimentary about my improved appearance. I was shocked to hear that during my absence we almost had a real tragedy, however. One night Joe took two common headache remedy pills and experienced a severe allergic reaction. He might easily have died alone in our home. It made us aware of how much we needed one another.

That evening we went to a football game with a group of friends, one of whom offered cookies with coffee on that very chilly night. I caught myself plotting to avoid eating a vanilla wafer, and I knew right then that I was still in trouble. The activities of the next day confirmed by suspicion. Joe bought sweet rolls for an afternoon snack. While he answered the telephone, I attempted to hide most of my uneaten roll under my napkin. Joe came back and discovered the hidden roll, and his optimism was quickly dissipated.

To one who has never had this sort of problem it is difficult to convey the threat presented by anything more caloric than lettuce. An entire sweet roll ranks about on par with an invading army. Add to that distortion the idea that someone with power is forcing you to succumb to the enemy. You can begin to imagine the problem.

Joe and I talked at length about this incident. I tried to explain how his attitude just made things worse—that my loss of autonomy, my feeling pressured to eat were inextricably linked to the illness I had. He took a more simplistic approach, saying that gaining weight was *the* answer.

For the next two weeks I went steadily downhill. On Sunday morning, November 16, Joe railed out at my breakfast of a slice of low-cal bread and tea. He was frustrated and worried beyond endurance. He made a piece of peanut butter toast but I could not, would not eat it. Although it is an emotional problem, anorexia has such obvious physical manifestations. You cannot camouflage a steadily wasting body and the reminder of the disease is in every look and touch.

We went to church that Sunday and immediately afterward Joe sent the girls home with a friend. He had decided to do something about my illness. He called both sets of parents. He asked his parents to come stay at our house and mine to meet us halfway to theirs. Bless their stalwart hearts. Both groups of parents came through again, willingly and quickly. Joe's parents rushed to get organized to leave their home and come to ours for an indefinite time. They were retired and therefore, luckily, free to leave, but even so it was a lot to ask. My parents met us and I went from Joe's car into theirs. As our cars went in opposite directions, I felt as if the core of me were congealing.

Again I experienced ambivalence. Partly it was so comforting to leave behind my responsibilities and go be a pampered little girl. On the other hand, I was seething at being yanked summarily out of my home. Now with hindsight, I can appreciate Joe's growing sense of panic as I continued to diet and exercise beyond reason. But at the time, I felt resentment and anger.

During the next three weeks at my parents' my mental health began to improve, although I did not gain much weight. I saw Dr. K. twice weekly and we talked about the problem but I found no insight at that point. Yet the clouds gradually parted and thoughts of *me* gave way to an occasional consideration of others. I shall never forget the evening my parents, my sister and I went Christmas shopping. For over an hour I was caught up in that task. It was amazing to realize how much time had lapsed with never a thought of a calorie!

But before I could enjoy the upsurge of that monumental evening, I had to plunge to the nadir of my existence.

We were emotional yo-yos at that point. I made well-intentioned resolves and spirits rose. Then I would regress and we went down. My sister Sarah arrived at our parents' on the Friday before Thanksgiving. She had driven several hundred miles to see me and attempt to talk sense to me. We had always been extremely close and listened to each other's advice. She suggested that I go home with her, then we would all come back for Thanksgiving. My resolve to eat and restore my health was strong. On Saturday I tried hard and family optimism rose.

Sarah and I left early on Sunday for the long drive to her home. Shortly after we arrived, even while Sarah was getting groceries and preparing dinner, I subjected myself to lengthy calisthenics. We can laugh now at that Sunday evening meal but it was rather grisly at the time. I attempted to hide a piece of chicken on my plate and later went almost into hysterics over a piece of raisin bread. Sarah talked to and soothed me as one would an overwrought child.

It was cold that November week but I still walked an hour or two a day while Sarah was teaching. Sarah prepared all sorts of taste-tempting tidbits, but I avoided them as one would plague.

On Wednesday afternoon as we were packing to return to Missouri, the very bottom seemed to drop out of my world. I was all alone—alone in someone else's house, my closest family far away. This realization tore me apart. Here were Bob and Sarah living such a normal, calm life. My husband, little girls, and parents-in-law were coping two hundred miles away from me, and the rest of my family was worried sick. I looked at myself in the mirror and truly abhorred what I saw. Yet I felt powerless to remedy the situation. I knew how to restore myself and return normality to our lives, but some demon gripped me and prevented improvement. Alone in the house I wept, pounded the floor, and gave way completely to utter despair and desolation. This was the emotional pit of my life.

Joe and the girls met us at my parents', and we shared Thanksgiving weekend. But Joe, dissatisfied with my lack of progress, insisted that I could not return home with them as planned.

What emotions did I feel? Frustration, anger, extreme longing for my daughters, a sense of isolation, all of these. But I also felt a sense of relief that I could go on being tended and cared for. Somehow I was freer at my parents'. It was Joe who loomed larger than life with the power to pull my strings and coerce me. My feelings toward him were hostile, but I felt them less when I stayed at my parents' house. In turn he experienced relief at not having to cope or look at me. He believed that if anyone could persuade me to snap out of this nightmare, my parents could.

For someone who craves security in routine and normality as I do, being away from my home, family, and work was a devastating blow. But I was not fit to return to my home or classroom. No one found it easy to be around me.

Daddy and I had always had an excellent relationship, so closely akin as we were in our thoughts and actions. Each of us was calm, deliberate, and even-keel, or at least I always had been. Neither of us was given to euphoria or depression. We both loved a few individuals intensely and were strong family people. For all these reasons I particularly regretted what my illness was doing to him. He stayed so calm and supportive, yet the experience took its toll. One remark revealed his pain—I remember it still.

Many days during my stay with them, I went to my parents' place of business. I partly offered to help, mainly I wanted to assuage my restlessness. One day a salesman came into the store, looked around, and left without even an introduction. Daddy remarked, almost in reverie, "You used to be so beautiful, and now..." His shame or embarrassment over me hurt deeply, though I clearly understood it then and now.

As I worked through the morass, it occurred to me that perhaps by striving to get to my absolute minimum weight, I was testing whether I was lovable and acceptable. Somehow, in the last few years before anorexia began, I had felt unaccomplished and unworthy, as if I had betrayed my earlier promise. Along with this sense of unworthiness came the need to reclaim control of my own destiny. Some part of me had thought that perhaps this extreme diet would give me the answers. It would reveal the core of me, virtually all that was left after dieting, and it would reveal whether I could pass muster. Certainly by controlling something as basic as eating, I proved that I alone was master of my own body. This idea explains one reason for my anorexia, although who can know for sure?

While my eating habits did not improve much, I began to feel measurably better. There were periods when my interest in the world around me grew, rather than just in myself. Life started to have its moments of contentment again. I thought I was making progress, a perceptible shift in thinking and feeling. But we still could not weigh or measure this change, and that was the kind of progress everyone else wanted. I had to quantify my improvement, and this I was not ready to do. No one believed me when I averred that I was better. An honest long distance call to a fellow teacher frightened her. With candor I admitted that gaining weight was still a problem but that I felt so much better, less harried and obsessed. She saw reason for alarm and in turn called Joe. Joe did not see it my way either and probably neither did my parents. Episodes of sneakiness and backsliding had abrogated most of the trust of the people I loved.

Poor Louise and Charles, my sister and brother-in-law, who lived in my home town near my parents. I spent many evenings with them, talking, listening, and being consoled. They were infinitely wise and endlessly patient and surely utterly bored with the whole thing.

But it was only when I sensed *myself* becoming bored with the issue of anorexia and the entire topic of my health that I saw a sure signal of a healthy return to emotional stability. For months I had reveled in being at center stage, a position secured by my increasingly skeletal state. But by early December I was sick of the whole thing. There was a *long* way to go to change my appearance, but I began to feel encouraged that my attitude had already changed. Events in the days that followed proved me wrong.

A week before Christmas break I went home. My parents-in-law needed to go home to take care of business and to prepare for the holiday. They were not young people or very healthy; still they had willingly undertaken the demands of my home, husband, and children. They offered only encouragement, never criticism or anger, and worked like yeomen in a difficult situation.

Back at home I plunged into whatever Christmas activities I could find to symbolize an everyday, ordinary family existence. I still was not eating much, and Joe became increasingly taciturn. No wonder, because I managed to do some woefully stupid things. For example, when we went Christmas shopping, I gravitated toward the book displays. But instead of browsing throughout the store for gifts, as I would have in the past, I immersed myself in diet books. When Joe saw me, it spoiled the evening.

Another incident, etched in our family history forever, was the "night of the diet cookies." You have no idea how much time and effort one can waste to cut corners calorically. Evening meals presented the problem. Throughout the day I could manage without eating and by spending hours in calisthenics or long walks. But dinner was the time of reckoning, when I had to cook and eat. One of my gems of subterfuge was a box of cookies I had cleverly purchased, or so I thought. They were diet cookies, small, thin, and rather tasteless, but cookies nonetheless. My plan was to serve the cookies, making it appear that my appetite was growing, while really I was still keeping close control of calories. To keep the plan a secret, I removed the cookies from the box, throwing that incriminating evidence away. I served the cookies attractively on a silver dish.

To anyone's tastebuds, those cookies were not treats. Joe is very bright, and he sensed my intentions. He asked to see the cookie package. I could not produce it except by sorting through the trash. Refusing, I finally admitted my secret about the diet cookies. At the end of his emotional tether, Joe picked up the dish and struck me over the head with it. In no way could such a small dish hurt, but the girls were horrified at this atypical physical display of anger. I tried to placate them and explain that their father was upset and worried. Now, many years later, we almost laugh about it, but then it was deadly serious.

Did I want to be caught up in such irrational activities? I do not know. I do know that these acts of bad judgment certainly were costly. No one honors integrity and honesty more than Joe. It takes him a long time to get over breaches of faith, but this was a quality that I loved and that attracted me early in our relationship. Certainly I could not fault him now, even though the disapproval was directed toward me.

The Christmas season had always been a special, luminous time for all of us. We always came together and celebrated with time-honored family traditions. This year we resolved to keep the holidays as usual, but in secret I was uptight at the thought of all the food and lack of opportunity to exercise. I worried over a way to avoid meals, especially those where Joe might be present.

One of the miserable experiences of my life was the ride to Missouri to begin the Christmas holiday. The car heater quit working and it was a raw, leaden-sky day. At that time I was constantly cold, no matter where I was. I had no body fat for insulation and my blood pressure was constantly low. Beyond that, the wall of cold between Joe and me was even more desolating. The girls, despite being young, sensed the undercurrents and Joe was perpetually distressed during those days. I was so miserable that I did not think we would ever get there. To top the matter, we stopped for lunch. I ordered the least possible, but even that loomed large to me.

Many people fantasize about being able to eat all they want, but it is impossible to portray the opposite condition. I had worked through my feelings far enough that I realized that my eating habits were only representative of the problem and not the problem itself. But to forego something as fundamental as eating presents the practical problems of malnutrition or starvation, and so what begins as a symptom eventually becomes the cause of even further problems.

We finally arrived in Missouri and the holidays began. By now I was quite adept in legerdemain. For instance, when I was in the house all alone, I would dump most of a half gallon of ice cream and then, when others returned, imply that I had eaten it. The story gave me an excuse to be too full to be hungry at mealtime. Or I would crumble cookies and send them down the garbage disposal, again for the same purpose. "O what a tangled web we weave when first we practice to deceive."

On Christmas Eve, as usual, we attended Midnight Mass at the impressive Christ Church in Joe's home parish. I dressed in a white winter suit and I looked absolutely hideous, as our family movies attest. People who had known me for years were flabbergasted at the change, just within the last year. Although I disliked being considered ugly, I delighted in being considered thin. The fact that "thin" had long ago become "emaciated" bothered me not at all.

On Christmas morning, I awakened with a determination to change, this time for sure. I would conquer this bugbear once and for all. Moderation was not possible. I began my all-out effort with hunks of pie for breakfast and proceeded to eat my way through the day. By the time we opened gifts Christmas night, I was a constipated, miserable mess. We all carried on, but the pictures show the strain. A lack of jollity is reflected in our eyes. Now I look back and regret my role in spoiling something as dear as the Christmas holidays.

A potential health problem appeared at this time. Even at times when I seriously wanted to eat, I frequently experienced pain and discomfort. Occasionally the distress became rather severe. Naturally everyone assumed this was another gambit to prevent eating, and at times I myself wondered whether this ailment might be psychosomatic indeed. Finally I resolved not to mention it. Maybe ignoring it would make it go away. Not until several years later was the pain diagnosed as pancreatitis, an inflammation of the important digestive gland, the pancreas. The pancreas works overtime when an individual eats rich or fatty foods. It is especially susceptible to damage from large amounts of food after periods of undernourishment. Research shows that pancreatitis is fairly common in recovered anorexics.

Many unfortunate ramifications arise when one goes off the deep end, as I surely had. The night before we were to return to our home, Joe and I insisted on taking my parents out to dinner as a thank-you gesture. It was a bitterly cold, icy night. Joe held on carefully to me, thinking that a hard fall could shatter my un-padded, highly exposed bones. Mother came tripping out at her usual quick pace and fell extremely hard. Plucky as she is, she insisted on still going out, but she was obviously in pain and very shaken up. It began to seem that my personal albatross would weigh down everyone closely connected with me.

We came back home and I insisted on returning to teaching. All along I pleaded with Joe that I would feel less freakish if only I could go back to work. He was adamantly opposed to my spending energy on anything but getting well. But I thought that resuming my regular life would facilitate the process. We compromised by agreeing to try it on a less than daily basis.

I called the headmaster/parish priest to inform him that I was home, this time for good, and ready to return to teaching. Going back to work was easier said than done, however. Father called back to insist that I stay home at least two more weeks and recuperate further. His intentions were both altruistic and practical. The students needed the continuity of one teacher and too many times had I come back only to leave school again. This inconsistency concerned the parents, too, and the school did not need upset parents.

Father suggested instead that I use the next two weeks to rest, read, and eat, and also to start seeing a physician whom he highly recommended. I knew Dr. G. from parish associations and respected him as a fine person. Although he was approaching retirement and was not taking new patients, he kindly agreed, as a personal favor to Father, to see me.

What a beautiful person Dr. G. was, outwardly and inwardly. Immediately he commanded my respect and trust. Here was someone in whom I could confide and really believe, medically and personally. His nurse was the same type of person, open and giving of herself in a way beyond that of a practitioner toward a patient.

Frankly, Dr. G. was aghast at the way I looked and at my skeletal body of eighty-eight pounds. As he examined me, he said that although he had helped liberate concentration camps during World War II, he had never seen anyone look much worse.

He asked a number of gently probing questions, helping me to think through my reactions to certain situations, past and present. He, like Dr. K. and Dr. J. before him, commented on my intelligence and apparent grasp of the problem. But I was still unaware that anorexia nervosa had been identified as an ailment that could strike others as well as myself. Intuitively, however, I sensed that I was approaching a turning point.

―――――――――

I wish that I could say that from then on the battle was all downhill. But that was not the case. I continued to be torn between the ever-increasing desire to be rid of this nightmare and the strong compulsion to submit to the hold it still had on me.

Dr. G. designed a medical treatment program for me that included weekly weigh-ins at the clinic and regular monitoring of my physical condition. He also suggested that I see a psychiatrist. Despite my aversion to the psychiatrist recommended by Dr. G. I kept the appointment. For several years I had heard rumors that this particular psychiatrist had a reputation for keeping his patients hospitalized inordinately long and for being rather brusque in manner; a totally unsympathetic individual.

Perhaps this preconception of Dr. R. clouded my judgment of him. But for whatever reason, I was absolutely certain that he was not for me. He immediately demanded hospitalization for an "indefinite but lengthy time." This was his opening statement, even before saying hello! When I replied that this approach seemed a bit summary, he informed me that he would have my husband on the phone before I got home and then "We'd see."

Needless to say, I was livid. I rose to the defensive, and for once I felt no threat. Anger completely crowded out any other emotion. His parting taunt—"You will never get better without hospitalization"—confirmed in me an iron-clad resolve to prove him wrong.

That single episode did as much to move me down the road to health as any other event. White-hot anger proved to be therapeutic. I had an ally at home, because Joe was not impressed by the rushed phone call from Dr. R. and was therefore willing to abide by my decision not to return to him.

I went regularly to see Dr. G. and he was kind enough to praise whatever weight gain I showed, all the while encouraging a greater effort. I had long since learned that bulking up shows up immediately on the scale. But if one does not sustain the effort, weight gain does not continue. It is possible to drink enough non-caloric liquids to show a gain, but the next week requires more intake just to stay even. Besides, I was nearing the point where deceptions were too much effort to maintain.

During the time before I went back to teaching, Joe insisted on preparing my breakfast every morning. I was still vacillating between wanting and not wanting to eat and during this interim I felt trapped and miserable. Some mornings I could do very well; others I could not, and the memory of those still chills me. On days when I woke up psychologically unable to eat what he had prepared, I had to devise ways to conceal the evidence. A fear lurked in me that he was watching from the other room instead of dressing to go to school. One morning my heart nearly stopped when he decided to have a cup of tea with me. I had dumped the oatmeal in the teapot! Just one time did he realize what I was doing, and he reacted with anger and hurt. He found the toast I had hidden after swearing that I had eaten it. After slapping me, he vowed to let me starve if that was my wish—a rare moment when Joe broke under the pressure. Throughout my illness, Joe was remarkably restrained, considering the stress of our lives. The only two remotely punitive physical encounters of our marriage came directly from the anorexic behavior. But even then, still no one had identified or explained to us that my actions were typical behavior of a known ailment. Surely such knowledge would have helped us understand and cope with each other.

Life limped along by fits and starts as I became more and more amenable to restoring my body and surrendering the love affair with being *thin*. At semester break in the middle of January I returned to my teaching. How good it seemed to be back on a schedule, doing all the normal things. On January 27, a day which is indelibly printed on my mind, I had an appointment with the director of the adult education classes which I had taught for several years.

Anorexics do not perceive their body images accurately. We simply do not view ourselves as the pitiful, almost grotesque embodiments of walking death that we appear to others. To us fat is the ultimate sin, with calories the sure-fire ticket to damnation. Bony is beautiful and the more bony the better. With this distorted perception of one's body, the anorexic persists in dieting long past the point of reason, past the point of being thin, sometimes to being ugly.

And ugly I was. First I weighed a shade over 80 pounds, nearly 50 pounds less than I had eight months ago. My menstrual periods had long since ceased and my hair was as dry and sparse as a very old person's might be. Despite all my calisthenics, muscle tone was poor because so much protein had been used for life-sustaining functions. My posture was terrible; I always slouched, because standing or walking tall siphoned off dwindling energy supplies. Almost no bones remained concealed. My tailbone hurt after short times seated because it was totally unpadded and still tender from the break the June before. My face had lines etched from chin to nose and cheekbones stood out prominently above sunken cheeks. My complexion was a dingy yellow, dry and lifeless. Smiling revealed equine teeth that appeared outsized in a fleshless face, a death mask grimace. No feature left resembled the person I had been. No wonder few recognized me.

As I dressed to run by the adult education office, I had to go to the laundry room to bring up some clothes. I glanced at my nude image in the full length mirror. I was stunned. For the first time I saw myself as everyone else was seeing me. I ran my hands over my body in horror as I discovered the disappearance of any buttocks. My body was virtually gone. Grabbing my clothes, I flew upstairs to the bathroom mirror to take a close look at my face. Again I felt revulsion as this yellow, aged skeleton looked back at me. I smiled, or so I thought, and was greeted by a pagan death mask. "What have you done to yourself?" I whispered to the mirrored reflection. Such ugliness was hard to accept.

For the first time throughout the entire ordeal I feared that I had crossed the brink irrevocably.

Suddenly I wanted to gain weight not because someone else had decreed it necessary, but because I saw the absolute necessity of it. "Please, God," I prayed, "don't let it be too late."

I dressed and rushed to the kitchen, where I began to eat with desperation. Lack of appetite was never the problem and once stimulated by food, I became overwhelmed by hunger.

En route to my appointment in adult education, I walked past a wall mirror in the office corridor. It reiterated the same grotesque ugliness that I had seen at home. The only remotely good thing was that twice in a row I recognized my body as the deformed creature it had become.

That evening I cooked a big chicken dinner and was still eating as Joe left for his graduate class. I told him that the time had come, but so often had I broken such promises that he remained impervious to my protestations of good faith.

But I meant my promise this time, more than ever before. Yet I was terrified of "ballooning": seeing a weight gain suddenly translated into huge, ill-proportioned basketballs of fat. The uninitiated cannot imagine the acute fear of ballooning that an anorexic experiences. Years later it is hard even for me to recall the near-terror that accompanied the ingestion of large amounts of food. The worry is that the weight gained will only go into one area, not evenly over the entire body. I feared that I would assume, at great magnification, the moon face or bloated stomach of a steroid user. I cannot recall with clarity the panic I experienced. It seems so ludicrous in retrospect, but seemed so compellingly real at the time.

So worried was I over ballooning that I called Dr. G.'s office and verbalized my concern. To her everlasting credit Betty, the nurse, was infinitely calm, patient, and medically reassuring, urging me only to eat as much as I could. She said she could guarantee that I would not balloon.

Eating large amounts of food slowly became an acceptable occurrence, but I decided not to eat frivolous junk food. Pop, candy, chips, things of that sort were self-indulgent and hard to justify. Also I realized that my body needed more than weight; it also needed an adequately balanced nutritional diet.

Joe insisted that to effect a cure I must also forego all organized exercise and calisthenics. He saw my compulsive exercises as part and parcel of the illness, and indeed they were. But on the other hand it seemed logical to me to try to keep firm and rebuild muscle tone as I gained. Therefore, I continued to exercise secretly.

When I went for my weekly check-up three days after my awakening experience, Dr. G. was pleased. My new eating habits were reflected on the scale and I was bubbling with resolve. We discussed the issue of exercise. Dr. G. cautioned against *all* exercise at this time. He explained that I needed to conserve energy whenever possible and had to interrupt the cycle of compulsive activity. I told him that my sit-up level was still at 1,000 per day, besides other activities. I explained the disagreement between Joe and me on that point. Dr. G. felt he should call Joe. Doubtlessly he acted on principle and out of concern for me when he called Joe, but I saw it then and still do as a breach of confidence.

Joe confronted me with what he had learned from Dr. G., and I promised to forego the exercise. That sacrifice provided a surprising amount of extra time for more profitable endeavors, such as reading stories with the girls or reading and working on my own projects. The old fear of ballooning died hard, however, and I was even more apprehensive without the security of calisthenics. Still the resolve lasted a week until Joe's birthday.

That morning I was scheduled for a second blood profile. It was another session where the attendant kept on stabbing because my veins were no better than they had been the August before. Finally it was over and I could go shop for birthday gifts. Our winter was mild that year and this was an unusually warm, sunny day. We had dinner reservations at a nice restaurant and plans for a movie afterwards. Knowing that we were going out somehow set up the old anxiety and I decided to do just a few exercises. As luck would have it, Joe saw me. He was not cross in any way but unknown to me he called Dr. J., the first psychiatrist I had seen. It seemed logical to Joe that I return to a psychiatrist who had some records of my illness. Joe also knew I considered Dr. J. reassuring and non-threatening.

By now my major concern was hearing whether my body had been damaged from August to February, the most intense months of severe nutritional deprivation. I was fearful that serious harm had occurred, but fortunately all was basically unharmed.

The next day I had my usual doctor's appointment and with high determination I revealed to Dr. G. my goal of 115 pounds by February 25. It was now February 12 and I was at 97 pounds. He cautioned me not to set unduly high goals and that approximately 4,000 calories daily would be about right, not the 7,000 I planned to try to eat. The reason for choosing February 25 was that it was my pay day and I wanted to buy a new wardrobe.

Perhaps I was ninety percent restored emotionally, but there were still some clouds. I interpreted Dr. G.'s "go slower" recommendation to mean that too rapid a gain would somehow be harmful. Subconsciously I began to footdrag a bit.

Meanwhile, at Joe's insistence, I returned to Dr. J. and we discussed the events of the last several months. Again, he believed me to be recovering well but suggested I see a therapist in his office, an individual with whom I felt instant rapport and trust. Sessions with this person were fruitful and satisfying. He made it an actual conversation with give-and-take. Without overt effort he helped me re-establish my dormant feelings of self-worth. I confided in him about the events in my life that had gnawed on me for years—gradually, insidiously eroding my zest for living. He helped me work through those episodes and by talking about them, put them into tolerable context. I also decided that living to please Joe placed an inordinate burden on him, one that he did not want or deserve.

Of course these realizations and changes did not occur overnight. February was a tug-of-war month, gaining two pounds and losing one. I didn't make my February 25 goal of 115 pounds. The last big confrontation that month occurred on February 27. The girls and I met Joe at his school gym to watch a wrestling match. After it was over, he made me weigh in, only to find that I had gained very little. He was unable to see that my attitude toward life was vastly improved and that a small gain was preferable to any amount lost. The symbol of my restoration to Joe was still that steady 115 pounds.

We had planned to go to Des Moines the next day for a state athletic tournament. Joe was opposed now to going believing that we could not have a good time. We did go, however, and made it through the day pleasantly enough though strained.

He used school as the leverage again. He demanded that I remain home until I could show some "meaningful progress." Again I felt like a trapped animal. I felt like he was trampling newly emerging spring flowers. I pleaded that rumors would be rife if I stayed away and that it would be unfair to my students.

Our own daughters had caught heavy colds and thus with honesty I could request a day home to care for them. Even then a few parents called that evening and I had to explain that I was not ill. The next morning I went back to school and did not miss another day all year.

Weekends are the customary high point of a working person's week. I had always happily anticipated weekends. Now that I was back to school I did not want weekends to come. Like holidays, Saturday and Sunday meant more family meal times and fewer opportunities to slacken my efforts at eating. Perhaps I wanted to gain weight—yes, surely I did—but it had to be done my way, in unsupervised situations. Eating or not eating still controlled my thoughts and actions. It was as foolish as compulsively concentrating on breathing. When weekends finally did become pleasurable again, I rejoiced in this symbol of returned mental health.

Joe and I began to work toward goals with friendly wagers. Pulling together on an end we agreed upon was beneficial to both of us. I set an upcoming Sunday as a target date to hit the 100-pound mark. As soon as church ended we went to the school gym to weigh in on the wrestling room scale. I showed 103 hard-won pounds. It is hard to say who was more elated, though each for different reasons. At least now I was in a safer weight zone, where an accident or illness would not be so devastating.

We took advantage of the spring-like weather that Sunday and went on a picnic with the girls. That evening Joe called both sets of parents, jubilant that one hurdle had been crossed.

I was still thin and gaunt, but there was a marked improvement. Fears of ballooning remained in my mind, though less severe and frequent. My attitude started to shift to a daring urgency: "Let's get on with this regardless." Whatever the consequences, I would gladly pay as we began to relax and trust one another again as a family. My wounds recovering, I was taking firmer steps by the day.

Periods of real progress and actual weight gain were interspersed with times of backsliding, slow gain or no gain at all. Longer and longer stretched the moments when I enjoyed a positive outlook and a general satisfaction with life. Out of the stranglehold of anorexia's compulsions, I experienced a feeling of near-euphoria most of the time. In other instances, surrendering thinness was still painful because it seemed to be an integral part of my being, more real and necessary than almost any other part. The struggle was wearisome, although it had become easier.

During the severe times of fall and early winter a day might loom ahead like a battle. There were so many adversaries—temptations to eat, no opportunity to exercise by the hour, exhortations from friends and family, the threat of possible hospitalization—all of these factors had to be conquered anew each day. Bedtime brought a temporary and welcome surcease. Frequently at bedtime Joe and I would talk, going through the process of seeking answers, but even then sleep eventually followed and with it, forgetfulness.

Anorexia is an insidious, ugly slave driver. It consumes its victim in proportion to how little the victim consumes. While the anorexic all but refuses to eat, she becomes obsessed with food and cookbooks. It is a great vicarious pleasure to concoct rich dishes for others to eat. Recipes become fascinating, and the ultimate in interesting reading are calorie-counting booklets. It is a rare anorexic who cannot spiel off the caloric value of almost any food.

Gradually, being told that I looked better became a compliment. For so long I had looked worse and worse. Had anyone ventured a compliment then, my reaction was immediate panic. I must be getting fat.

Desperation may breed boldness. I, naturally reticent, deigned to ask others their weight, trying to figure out where I fit in. If a woman looked slim and firm, about my height, and weighed more than 115, then I felt some reassurance that maybe I could weigh that much without being hideously blubbery.

Where does common sense go in the anorexic? Our reasoning capacity about any bodily issue is gone. The best arguments of reason, medicine, or memory count for nothing. To allow oneself to be persuaded otherwise is to abandon that all-important control. Being in control is absolutely paramount to the anorexic, and the most fundamental place to start is with one's own body.

My theory is that the anorexic either recovers to an extent or dies, either of starvation or the boredom of self-focus. It finally becomes such drudgery to concentrate only on oneself or a rehash of consumed calories, that one gradually weans herself away.

The effect of proper nourishment on my life was astonishing. As I ate correctly and filled out, it was comparable to watering a dehydrated plant. I was not blooming yet, but there was a vitality and ripening that had not been seen for a long time.

The legacy of mistrust and doubt I had created in my family died hard, however. Those closest to me were aware of the nuances of my eating. Quite assuredly they counted, weighed and measured in a glance every portion I took or, worse yet, did not take. Even a ravenous eater finds it difficult to enjoy food under those conditions, but observation is a price the anorexic pays.

We went home for Easter that year. Joe, my mother, and I went shopping for my new wardrobe, although my weight was still several pounds below 115. I recall the pleasure of trying on, modeling, and selecting bright, attractive clothes after months of being swallowed up in the old clothes which hung on me, scarecrow-fashion. One of the thrills of having anorexia is the satisfaction of wearing all your clothes too large. Any baggy garment attests to the success of one's diet. By early April, however, I was ready for a wardrobe that fit.

Admittedly my appearance was much improved. But looking now at pictures from back then, I realize that even at that juncture there was vast room for growth. My legs still looked like pipe stems. Apparently depleted muscle mass does not rejuvenate over a short time. For a while I chose short skirts and dresses, basking in my newly awakened physical self. Carefully I avoided anything that might feel tight, however, still following that habit of liking to feel clothes hanging on me. Goodness knows I was conscious of my waistline and abdomen.

In many ways anorexia is stronger than grief, more abiding than love. I have experienced all three and it almost seems that the illness outlasts the others. That obsession does not easily relinquish its hold. Even in sorrow one finds temporary lulls that gradually lengthen, but anorexia makes an omnipresent companion.

How very many occasions did it spoil. In August of 1969 my sister took the girls home with her for a week—a summer custom, enjoyed by adults and children alike. When it was time to pick them up, I took a train to Kearney. Ordinarily my sister and I would have a wonderful visit, but it was different on this trip. Would I resist the summer food and ice cream parlor excursions? And then the oft-repeated question, Why did I feel that I had to forego such simple pleasures?

It was a strained few days because of my wet blanket tactics. Sarah had some friends in to meet me and visit, but my only contribution was to worry about eating refreshments. We went shopping and I tried on a black outfit. Its effect was to emphasize my stooped, angular body and white, lusterless skin. We agreed that nothing was becoming, and tacitly we knew why.

Sarah and I talked at length. She suggested that I see her physician, a doctor in whom she had great confidence. He concluded that I was intelligent, needed to gain a few pounds and perhaps take vitamins. He never mentioned anorexia. I truly believe that in 1969 few physicians had seen or studied cases of anorexia. I *knew* that something was wrong, but no one could tell me what. How much it would have meant had any doctor, or anyone else, diagnosed my trouble, explained the symptoms, and discussed the probable time it would run. It was patently evident that something was wrong. But what?

Joe reacted to that doctor's visit with disapproval. He felt that he knew the answer to my foolishness. Even now he laments taking that stand, not realizing that I was sick, not stubborn. Yet he was no more ignorant than anyone else I encountered.

To a teetotaler an alcoholic is an enigma. It appears so easy to forego drinking. Perhaps we are more patient now with smokers, drinkers, and gamblers as we learn more about the causes of their afflictions, but hunger is such a basic drive that self-denial of food is difficult to fathom. To the overweight who must diet, surely the anorexic must seem a most unsympathetic character. Yet to one who has wept over eating a forkful of scrambled eggs, let me assure you that eating can be its own hell.

These digressions are important in depicting the picture of an anorexia sufferer. Surprisingly, most follow the same pattern, and to observe one is to see them all. If I had realized that I had fellow sufferers dieting and exercising along with me, some of the allure of my compulsions would have vanished. By being the *only* one to become spectrally thin, I craved uniqueness and commanded attention. I might have laughed a little at the ideas of numbers of us doing the same thing. Of course that is a moot question and I can only reflect from the advantage of elapsed time.

Easter was especially meaningful in 1970. It was as if I had undergone my own resurrection and the spring was bringing personal rebirth. How rewarding it was to have some breathing space in the fight. And a fight it was, every mouthful of the way.

Early in May I reached 110 pounds and decided that I had arrived. Yes, it was short of the 115 we agreed on but well within a safe zone. Perhaps by reneging just a little I was retaining some final control over my life. The day I reached the 110-pound status I felt as if a weight were lifted off of me. I did not appear fat, had not ballooned on the way up, and was quite respectable-looking. Talk about being lighthearted. We had a parents' meeting at school that night. I approached it eagerly, sure that the pitying, puzzled looks would be gone for good. That was pretty much true and for that I was grateful.

Joe's reaction was not quite as positive when I told him that I had reached 110 and that was where I intended to stay. He acceded that the recovery was remarkable and that I was light-years improved. But he also insisted that I still was not finished, nor was I as attractive as I could be.

The question of whom to please again surfaced strongly. Having learned early that one's word was a bond, I knew that I had not fulfilled my promise. It still seemed a small point to push, but we did. He had reservations that I could make the final push. Deep down, so did I.

In comparison with emotional ailments physical illnesses seem far preferable, mainly because there are nice tidy endings. Either you recover or you die, by and large. But, as I discovered with anorexia, there is no one time that the sufferer can say, "That's over and done with; now on to something else." Even when the

basic problem is alleviated, scar tissue remains. Pain keeps returning to the victim and to the family involved. For several years Joe
experienced flashbacks in the form of unbidden memories of the
way I looked at my worst. Such unsolicited pictures could spoil
the current moment, regardless of how unrelated it was to the
problems of the past.

Throughout the difficult times I refused to believe that I had
an endless problem. I was steadfastly convinced that there were
answers somewhere that would unlock these chains. But why
couldn't someone please tell me what was wrong?

And yet the bonds did hold, and hold, and hold. Very often,
especially in the spring of 1970, I came so close to 115 only to lose
my grip and slide back down. It was as if an invisible force were
working to prevent my victory.

A natural reaction to the inexplicable is frustration. Watching
someone *nearly* make a goal and then swerve at the last moment
can anger and disgust the onlooker, especially an individual who is
close to the situation, and hopes for the achievement of that goal
for himself too.

But even as regression occurred, definite signs of progress kept
developing. I no longer contrived ways to try out department
store display scales whenever I saw them. That had been one of
my habits during the early days of anorexia. If I got into a store
where it was possible to try out the scales, off would come the
shoes and onto the scale I would go. You would be surprised at
how many different readings the various scales provided. While
trying on or otherwise sampling goods for sale is common enough,
trying out scales must be surely unusual.

Of course dining out and deliberately dropping one's food is
rather bizarre too. One way I found to survive meal times in my
worst stages was to urge dining out with other couples, the more
the better. First, being with others helped alleviate the pressure of
family meals. Secondly, it was far easier to waste as much food as
possible surreptitiously. Food could be folded into paper napkins
and kicked unobtrusively out of sight or dropped onto the floor.
This practice is representative of the desperation the anorexic experiences when she is confronted with food. Personally, littering is

abhorrent to me, as is any other wasteful, inconsiderate practice. Nevertheless, I am guilty of just such behavior, perpetrated (I thought) in self-defense.

In the aftermath, my family wondered whether they should have insisted on hospitalization to force nourishment. From a purely physiological view such practice might have been temporarily beneficial. But emotionally, the results would have been devastating.

Anorexics maintain such rigid diets in order to assert control. So practices that minimize that feeling of self-possession just evoke intensified rebellion. I can remember clearly the more ardent attempts to persuade me to eat, and how those efforts just drove me to eat less.

Sometimes I wish it were possible for adversaries to enter into the minds of the other side and exchange points of view. The people most involved in anorexia are decidedly adversaries in a war. The anorexic herself is on one side and all others conspiring to help her are the enemy. Often the frustration a family feels toward the anorexic is so great that she almost becomes an evil force to them. It is incomprehensible to the uninitiated that anyone would starve willfully. But on the other hand, the anorexic's terror over food is equally misunderstood. Yet how frightening and maddening it must be to watch a loved one slowly but surely slip away, when simply eating would cure the problem. Or so it must seem.

Simply eating will not cure the malady, and families must understand that. I tried to communicate this idea to my worried family on many occasions. That I was progressing, even before I started eating, became abundantly clear in my mind but it was hard to convey to others.

Thus it was in my quest for those final few pounds. The urgings and exhortations to "push a little harder" competed with my attitude. "I've come so far; accept and be grateful," I wanted to say. Joe interpreted the last bastion of will as obstinancy or evidence that I was still sick. In my mind it meant that a very small portion of the battlefield was still reserved for me exclusively.

Perhaps the younger anorexic is influenced strongly by the current preoccupation with beautiful, sleek, sexually alluring bodies.

Modern society often appears to equate fat with sin, or at least sinful self-indulgence. Our media glorify the body beautiful and usually that body is slender. The vital statistics of beauty contestants lead one to believe that true comeliness can only be 5'9" and weigh 109 pounds, which somehow stacks up elegantly on these girls. For most of us the same size might not be as glamorous, but we infer that it would be.

Young boys, on the other hand, have heroes of grander proportions to emulate. We are impressed by the heft of the bodybuilder; thus teenage boys can take pride in being large. From the earliest days of infancy proud parents are jubilant over their big boy babies while girls are described affectionately as dainty and petite. From the first, our society prescribes the desired shape and size for each gender.

Theorists also suggest that anorexia typically strikes young girls who cannot deal with their emerging womanhood and seek to keep their bodies childish. Anorexia is one way they find to reach that goal. Curves disappear, bones protrude, menses stop. And there is little excess energy to direct toward sexual encounters.

Yet I flew in the face of this theory. I was twenty-seven, not seventeen; happily married and a loving mother. Right now in my small home town a woman older than I appears to me to be anorexic. Perhaps we need to up-scale the ages included in our picture of anorexia victims in order to diagnose and treat everyone properly.

I was still struggling in May to hit that magic number so I could "let it end forever." I hadn't yet stayed at 115. Finally, Joe equated my slow progress with obstreperousness. He gave me the ultimatum that moved the mountain.

I remember that we were sitting in the living room on a cloudy Friday afternoon. We were trying to talk over why I didn't seem to gain those last few pounds. Discussions were going nowhere and both of us were heartily fed up with the whole thing. "All right," he told me, "you can starve if that's what you want, but I guarantee you that I'll leave and take the girls." The remotest prospect of losing my daughters penetrated the last wall of resistance. I knew that this was not an idle threat, and I knew I would lose all I loved if it happened. My recent behavior would demonstrate instability to any judge. Yes, I could lose the little girls whom I adored.

Frankly, I think that by this point I was sufficiently recovered to *want* some prodding. Now I could justify indulgent calorie consumption to gain weight. Gaining weight had a positive purpose, and thus I could accept the goal. Six months earlier I would have panicked but persisted in my anorexic pattern. But I was ready to take the final step. Within a short time I gained the additional pounds, and even I had to admit that they were an improvement.

To celebrate, we took a weekend trip with friends and I bought a new outfit. My hair was soft, thick, and lively again, whereas before it had been thin and dull—the hair of a sick, old woman. Amazingly, almost all physical manifestations were erased . It was fun to be attractive again and not a zombie. The best part was that my body image perception was accurate enough for the first time in a long time to view myself objectively.

Did the whole unfortunate episode end right there? Did we all live happily ever after? No, to both questions.

An experience as intense as anorexia sears its victims and leaves them with residual damage. For the family it leaves behind a legacy of distrust, tension, and fear. For the victim it leaves behind ingrained thought patterns that are hard to break. Even when restored common sense says that we look better, we are healthier and happier at a more normal weight, there is still that allure of thinness. The flirtation with the downward side of the scale dial never ceases. If we gained enough to reach the prescribed goal, the nagging suspicion that we overly compromised remains.

Newly recovered emotional health is as tentative and fragile as a spring bud. It can be frost-nipped so quickly, or it can be coaxed into full blossom. Just as a parent may continue to monitor a once-ill child, so does the family watch over the recovered anorexic. This attention creates some stress, of course, because it keeps food and eating in a spotlight rather than letting them become normal, incidental aspects of life.

As many times as my well-meaning family urged me to join them in having a piece of pie or a dish of ice cream, no one ever invited me to have just a salad. The family thinks their goal is to get calories into the dieter—understandable, but I would recommend a less overwhelming first step. Well-intentioned actions, liberally laced with desperation, are often tinder near an open fire.

Of course it is maddening to see a wasted creature select the driest, least caloric morsel on a dessert tray, but to choose and then eat it represents a real victory for the anorexic.

For the victim always operates from a position of weakness. She must cultivate a cunning born of desperation to get through the day her way. Her weakness is not necessarily physical lassitude, but rather defensiveness, born of being in the wrong.

To prepare to write this account of my own bout with anorexia, I re-read my diary of those days. The entries begin only after recovery was underway but, even so, vulnerability surfaces on its shaky legs.

The entries of the spring and summer months of 1970 show an almost pathetic need to please and prove myself. I was miserable, worrying whether the doctor would be satisfied with the gain for the week and whether Joe would realize and accept my good intentions. There was a note of exultation when these influential figures were happy with my efforts. Ultimately the power brokers had the final say. They must, or the anorexic must sever all ties and become a compulsive recluse.

The loss of my independence weighed heavily on me. The very means I used to assert self-control and dominance in my life— my diet—became the instrument by which I lost those powers. Frankly, there is no happy solution to this dilemma, and it goes to the depth of the problem. If the anorexic is left unpressured to improve, I believe fervently that she will stay on the treadmill unto death. At least I would have. It is a volcanic situation for the family, as well as for the victim.

The image of a seesaw comes to mind. First one side is up, and then the other. It is almost impossible to maintain balance at the mid-point. Now, years later, I can project one of my daughters into the same situation and feel the panic that would envelop me. No wonder my family suffered. Now I can share their point of view, but they will never fit into the shell of my fears during that time unless, God forbid, they too become anorexic.

Perhaps there is some poetic justice in my being a victim of an emotional problem. Up to that point I had empathized little with those who had problems, believing that anyone could conquer emotional difficulties. He or she just had to try hard enough and would just snap out of it.

I have changed this attitude after struggling with my own problem. Now I can remember all too well the times of seeming hopelessness and rock-ribbed despair, the days that the solution was quite clear and yet I could not force myself to accept it. Finally, of course, one must recover. For the anorexic, that recovery has to come from within oneself.

The therapist helped me realize that my rebellion was a giant step toward breaking the mold of impossibly high standards, rigidly set. So long as I was trying to be what I perceived others expected of me, I could never be free of pressure or resentment. Admittedly anorexia is an extreme way to rebel, but the restructuring of one's self-assurance and coping mechanism sometimes requires a dramatic change.

To this day I do not feel that others, namely family members, foisted ultra-high goals on me. Most of my aims were self-imposed. I place no blame on my parents or anyone else for those elevated aspirations and strict self-discipline. I am equally sure that I internalized the values of those closest to me, and indeed, the standards of my family were high. Early on we children observed little patience in our parents with slipshod efforts or easy compromises. The major mechanism of discipline, as I grew up, came from each of us striving to meet certain expectations. I enjoyed success then, complete with the comfort of knowing what behavior was expected in a given situation. Lines were more clearly drawn then for everyone than they are now. Who could predict that occasionally someone such as I would go overboard and turn guidelines into nooses?

Since 1970, my life has had its ups and downs. I would like to say that the problem ended when I attained my weight goal and that from then on, all vestiges of anorexia were gone. But that is not the truth. In fact, I wonder whether a recovered anorexic is not rather like a recovered alcoholic. One can remain on the wagon for years but the potential to slip is ever-present.

I have played the brinkmanship game several times since over the years. Usually the episodes occurred during a time of stress, associated with a situation I could not control. The urge remains to retreat, using my body as leverage. If the external environment will not be manipulated, then I can surely control my physical self.

I used such behavior if I wanted to punish Joe for some transgression, such as an investment I considered unsound or a family scene in which I felt he was too dominant. I fully realize the effect my excessive dieting can have on my husband. Lately, fortuitously, I have come to consider this type of childishness totally counterproductive, and I truly believe that I shall never resort to it again. I fervently hope not.

The anorexic is not striking out at an individual so much as she is at a situation, something she sees as an obstacle that she cannot control. I am vindictive, not against Joe the person, but against the loss of freedom, the necessity of marital compromise that he represents. Like most other anorexics, I am not a compromiser by nature.

I still find it gratifying to lose weight, and I still much prefer to find myself lighter come morning than heavier. Even now a weight loss confirms that I have controlled the self-indulgence equated with overeating. Somehow I have resisted the temptation that entraps "lesser" (fatter) mortals.

But I have learned to limit my will to shed pounds, as much because of what it did to others as what it did to myself. The willful anorexic does notice how her own excessive behavior is at the apex of self-indulgence. She thinks she is gaining in control, but the more she seeks to control her body by rigid dieting and exercise, the less she is actually in command of her own destiny. We anorexics learn that lesson very slowly and painfully, though.

There were times when I gained enough weight to return temporarily to dieting. At first it was almost amusing to actually need to lose a few pounds. But soon dieting to lose eight or ten pounds becomes a tedious—and frightening—proposition. Once I was down where I should be, I might decide to go on with it.

Strangely there seems to be an internal mechanism that now even decrees to me when enough is enough. That threshold level is somewhat below the promised weight of 115, but still I shrink from going much lower than that. When I do, my energy level decreases and I look unattractive. Joe can tell almost to the pound and he begins to exert a subtle pressure. Is he still sensitive and apprehensive? Yes, definitely, and he will be for a long time.

Only once in recent years have I gone significantly below my own limit. Several factors entered in: a long, exhausting winter; a demanding spring; and anger over some unnecessary economic reversals.

Usually I heed the warning signals of the gathering storm, which come in the form of questions. "Are you watching your weight pretty closely?" "Do we have any ice cream?" A bit later, "How much *do* you weigh now?" I also feel his hands pause over any bony protuberances on my body. He becomes reserved and terse. Before, under such circumstances, I would feel trapped and start eating, to keep our lives on an even keel. Yet this time I disregarded the clues.

The explosion occurred on a beautiful early May Thursday. He marched me upstairs and ordered me to disrobe and weigh. When he saw the scale register 106, we started again through questions and stormy recriminations. He was furious and upset and I became the apologetic, defensive creature of old. Again he gave me orders. One, I was to call in sick, as I indeed was in his estimation, and stay home for several days to eat and rest. Second, I was not to touch the lawn mower or do anything physical until I came to my senses.

Again I am not sure that I did not think deep down that I was caught up anew on the same old treadmill, secretly waiting for

Joe to intervene. Anyway, I repented the error of my ways and fell to repairing the situation with gusto. I did refuse to stay away from work and shortly this crisis ended. It was the last of any magnitude.

I still watch what I eat, though less and less as time passes. My eating habits are deplorable. For example, I am an habitual nibbler. I will eat a cookie by halves or quarters rather than entirely. I prefer meal portions that are small, but between dinner and bedtime I will pick and snack constantly. It is easier for me to eat three bowls of cereal one-third full rather than one full bowl at a sitting. My rational mind says this is illogical, but emotionally I operate this way.

Occasionally I still go on binges, but they hold no terror and rarely even create physical discomfort. Perhaps a metabolic trigger controls my periodic carbohydrate urges. Certainly stress invariably triggers an eating jag. I recognize these patterns and some day may decide to work through and alter them further. But perhaps not. I really have to work to muster the feelings of self-loathing that used to accompany binging. There has not been a laxative in the house for years.

The months of fanatic calorie counting come in handy if anyone wants to know the caloric value of almost any food, because I certainly do remember. And, yes, I still count them more often than not.

I believe that my compulsive drive to be perfect and accomplish superhuman feats has diminished almost to extinction. With Emily Dickinson, I can say without pain, "I'm nobody. Who are you? Are you nobody too...?" And yet even as I write I am belying this, for is not writing a form of ego-stroking? I will soon have my Ph.D., still another way to say, "Let me *prove* I am exceptional." Still, within my own conscious awareness, I am more content just to *be*, to smell the roses on the way to wherever, than I have ever felt before.

While still preferring slim to plump, I didn't take to the grapefruit and egg diet that Joe and I went on one recent summer. I could not wait to be done with that. Where once there was a great, gaping chasm of compulsion and despair, now there is a tiny cavity-sized sore spot to tease lightly with my tongue as one does a sensitive tooth.

Gradually eating has become for me what it is for non-anorexics, namely, a necessity and a pleasure. We are a diet-conscious society, worshipping the body beautiful. And I am part of that society, in the mainstream. You cannot imagine the ultimate isolation of running so hard in a different direction. It may well be the most exhausting battle of my life.

Losing first my beloved father and then Joe's parents, whom I also loved, were deep sorrows, but I worked through them without the curse rearing its ugly head. Even the pain that accompanied those losses could not match the anguish of and confusion of anorexia when I did not even know what was wrong or why.

Without doubt I am a stronger person for having experienced an emotional problem. I can now draw upon the strength of self-understanding and acceptance. I can work within the boundaries of my own limitations without feeling disgusted with my imperfections.

My girlhood statement that I would rather be dead than mediocre is no longer true. Life now, in early mid-years, is rewarding as I live it. The necessity of proving myself exists no more in its painful, dictatorial form.

―――――――――――

Years ago in high school Spanish we learned the phrase, "*Yo soy Yo*," a most emphatic way of saying "I am I!" And thus it is now with me. I believe I have earned the right to say that this person is who I am—not perfect, not exceptional, but a special individual nevertheless, as is each person.

To the family or friends of an anorexic sufferer, may I suggest several things? Foremost, help the victim identify the ailment. Do not let her suffer a nameless terror. It was my own reading, that began five years ago, that *finally* informed me that anorexia nervosa existed.

Seek as much clinical information as you can to learn the typical course of the disease. Your understanding will enable you to practice the endless patience that you must display. Show your concern, anger, and frustration, but keep your emotions confined and managed. The anorexic is confused and miserable enough already without your heaping your own fears and pain on her. Of course it is a tough duty, but patient understanding will help her the most.

Be as supportive as you can be and listen to her multitude of eating-related fears ridiculous though you know them to be. She needs reassurance and comfort.

Do not hesitate to get qualified medical treatment. She will need physical care and certainly some assistance in working through the psychological ramifications of anorexia. Do make absolutely certain that she is in the care of the *right* psychologist or psychiatrist. Ask your family doctor, school nurse (if the patient is in school), or nutritionist to recommend psychiatrists or psychologists. Do not hesitate to ask about his or her experience in treating anorexia. It is invaluable to find someone who understands anorexia. Very likely there will be family sessions, because anorexia is not the problem of the anorexic alone.

It does no earthly good to ask her if she knows how bad she looks. I assure you, she does not. A distorted body image is central to the psychology of the anorexia sufferer. Nor does she regard her bony, malnourished body as ugly, even if she can acknowledge its emaciated state. She constantly sees thinness as an elusive goal yet to be reached, not the state which she has attained.

Do not force her to eat. At critical points, forcing food may be medically necessary. But I believe that lay efforts to force-feed, however well-intentioned, only solidify an anorexic's determination to outwit others' efforts. If anything, forcing her will intensify her efforts to avoid eating. Do try to get her to join you or you join her in a non-threatening snack or meal. You may consider it pathetically meager, but every little bit helps. By sharing her meal with you she will feel less unacceptable.

It really is fruitless, at first anyway, to ask her why she is doing this, because most likely she cannot tell you. Yes, she knows she wants to lose weight. But she does not know what compels her to lose long after the real need to diet is gone. Only as she works through the problem can she articulate the deep-seated reasons.

As a concerned person you are on a tightrope, trying to balance between crowding her to the limit or ignoring the problem until she is destroyed. Left alone I do not know which would have come first, working through my problem successfully or starving to death. It creates a most difficult situation for loved ones.

Be aware that recovery is not instantaneous, even when it once begins. There will be regressions and breaches of your trust, but she will not enjoy those times any more than you do.

My personal experience was that anorexia is better treated by allowing the pursuit of normal, everyday activities. I always made better emotional progress when I was doing customary, routine things.

On one point perhaps medical authorities will disagree with me. But I would confront the victim and say, "Look, I know you will hide food, induce vomiting, and generally resort to all sorts of subterfuge to avoid eating. Let's just save your time and energy and not waste the food in the first place." At least this attitude gives her an out, allows her to eat less without subterfuge, and is physically less dangerous than the gagging or laxative routines.

Verbal browbeating and derision serve no purpose, except to reinforce the anorexic's negative self-image. She is a victim just as much as a sufferer of appendicitis. Yet we still see the anorexic as willfully self-destructive and, probably, inordinately obstinate. But ascribing willfulness to the victim of an illness is a judgment that is inaccurate and unfair. Goodness knows she would be whole and healthy if she could be. Yes, I know, many think that she could remedy the entire situation if only she would eat! And if she were not obviously very intelligent, you would question her mentality. But that intelligence ought to be a clue as to how penetrating this illness really is.

The typical anorexic will be much younger than I was, so her family can exert more control and influence over her. Some research indicates that the younger the onset occurs, the better the chance of complete recovery.

In case you wonder why I have only used the feminine pronoun in my descriptions of anorexics, let me assure you I have a sound reason. The problem seems to be gender-linked and very predominantly female, so it is fair to assume that just about every anorexic out there is female.

Perhaps the name should be changed. *Anorexia* means "loss of appetite." At least in my experience, however, the *appetite* remained but the *will* to eat was suppressed. In other words, the illness goes beyond the appetite. An anorexic must work through the circumstances of her ailment until she recognizes that her habit of not eating is *not* the central problem, although it probably seems so to observers. Only after she perceives her desire to lose weight in a totally different light, as a symbolic act toward herself and her loved ones, will she begin to recover. Only then can she give in to and admit normal hunger once again.

It was months or years before I would allow myself to say that I was hungry. Somehow before that I feared that was conceding too much. Nor did I admit that I was ever tired. Physical needs were beyond the pale of my acceptance. What sheer relief it is to own up to such normal physiological conditions as hunger and weariness. We count victory in small ways at times.

If possible, the family of the anorexic should try to avoid becoming obsessed with the problem. The victim's obsession is enough. Do not let the illness become the core of your existence too. With family counseling, an integral part of some treatment programs, adjustments in behaviors and interactions might be asked of others, too. These details will vary, of course, with each family, with each individual suffering through.

Almost any adversity can strengthen bonds if those involved are willing to struggle and eventually triumph together. Even anorexia—persistent, disorganizing, ever-apparent—can serve this strengthening purpose. I know it seems impossible at the time. Months and years of discouragement erode deeply, but the victory is as sweet as any one can ever achieve. I know. My family and I have been there—and back.

PART 3
Research and Treatment

Introduction

An explanation is in order for Part III. After the personal revelations in the book, this research section may seem cold and clinical. The information is not meant to be frightening or unfeeling. Instead, I am offering this to you in the hope that you will find some needed explanations and come away more knowledgeable; able to get help, either for yourself or your loved one.

Several times I have mentioned the almost desperate desire I experienced in wanting anorexia nervosa identified. It was as if a veil had lifted when I began to read about the subject and realize there was a sisterhood of beleaguered sufferers. Knowledge gave me weapons to continue my personal battle. Perhaps you too will benefit from understanding.

The anorexic is often mistrustful, sure that she is being manipulated to gain weight or lose control of her own body. However, if she can read the results of dispassionate research, she will come closer to believing the truth about her disease. Cold, objective facts may make an impact, whereas impassioned pleading of loved ones will not.

There are some technical terms in Part III, but they appear so often in the literature that it seems unfair to omit them. I have also referred to *bulimia* and the *binge-purge* syndrome. My apology is for the lack of attention to this area now recognized as a serious eating disorder.

For the sake of definition, let us regard bulimia as compulsive overeating. It is a condition in which the sufferer may consume 4,000 to 50,000 (!) calories within a few hours. This is binge eating and may be followed by purging the body of unwanted food through forced vomiting or use of laxatives. The bulimic may be of normal weight or overweight. It is not uncommon for the anorexic to binge-purge at least occasionally. Anyone with such symptoms needs professional help at once.

I say that anorexia is no longer a factor in my life. I lie. This book is testimony that anorexia and I are inextricably linked. Much of the research in Part III appears in my doctoral dissertation on anorexia nervosa, and I spend numerous hours where I teach listening to young people talk to me about their struggles with anorexia. I was seared with the flame of anorexia but, happily the results led to the discovery of greater strength, self-knowledge, and self-acceptance.

If anyone else can come to understand and work through this illness, in part because of what I have written, my pain will have been well used. Accept Part III as it is offered, a summary of research that will aid in understanding anorexia nervosa. It is through understanding that wisdom finally comes.

Research and Treatment

Anorexia nervosa is an eating disorder approaching epidemic proportions. Crisp (1982), in a study of British school girls, found anorexia nervosa in one of every 100 females aged 16 to 18 years. While once considered to be a rare disorder, anorexia currently appears rather prevalent, especially among adolescent girls (Bruch, 1978; Crisp, Palmer and Kalway, 1976). Levenkron (1982) estimates that at least 150,000 American women, aged 12 to 25 years, suffer from anorexia nervosa. These figures do not include such related eating disorders as bulimia, the victims of which would raise substantially the number of afflicted women. An information-clearing house, Anorexia Nervosa and Related Disorders, has recently been established. Its statistics corroborate the increasing incidence of anorexia nervosa.

If diagnosed cases are increasing in the United States and England, the same is true also of other Western populations, including those of Sweden, Scotland, and Australia. Incidences are reported in the Soviet Union, the Arab/Moslem world, and eastern European countries as well.

The anorexia nervosa phenomenon, virtually exploding in frequency today, appears to exist only in societies affluent enough to feed their people. Sours (1980) pointed out that cultural and social influences loom large in today's increased number of cases of anorexia. When food is readily available, it becomes symbolic of other things. In areas where survival is a struggle, anorexia is rare.

Despite its rapid increase globally, anorexia is not a new disorder. Indeed, as Sours wrote in *Starving to Death in a Sea of Objects*, allusions to anorexia nervosa began in the third century A.D. The first well-described clinical case was reported over a thousand years ago.

The best-known early description of anorexia nervosa was written by Richard Morton (1689), whose study most contemporary experts consider a landmark diagnosis. Morton noted many

or all of the essential features of the illness. He described amenorrhea, loss of appetite, weight decline, constipation, almost frenzied attention to studies, and subnormal body temperature. These
same symptoms are hallmark points observed in diagnosing anorexia today.

Gull (1874) and Lasèque (1873) studied and reported on incidences of anorexia nervosa at about the same time. Both related
the problem to gastric nervous malfunction reflected as a repugnance for food. Gull first named this eating disorder "apepsia hysteria." In modern terms that means a "nervous stomach" that does
not secrete the digestive juice pepsin. This malfunction leads to
loss of appetite and a feeling of repugnance for food. However,
upon discovering pepsin in the stomachs of anorexics (as well as
occurrences in males), Gull renamed the disturbance "anorexia
nervosa" and searched for psychopathological factors. Anorexia
nervosa means a loss of appetite (anorexia) through a nervous inability to eat. We now know that anorexia is wrongly named.
Appetite is keen.

Lasèque, working concurrently though independently of Gull,
concluded that "hysterical anorexia" was related to gastrointes-
tinal tract problems and advocated changing the description to in-
anition—exhaustion through starvation.

Another French physician, Huchard (1883), observed that pa-
ralysis, anesthesis, and blindness—frequent in hysteria—were
missing in anorexia nervosa. Therefore, Huchard suggested that
Lasèque's term "anorexia hysterique" be renamed "anorexia men-
tale," the term now used in France.

Freud (1912), Janet (1929), Binswenger (1944), and others expressed diagnostic opinions about this baffling phenomenon.
Opinions varied as to preferred course of treatment, causative factors, primary and secondary symptoms, and whether the ailment
was primarily physiological or psychological.

This latter question evolved logically from the direction diagnosis took early in the twentieth century. It was then that the Ger-
man pathologist, Morris Simmonds (1914), made clinical and
anatomical observations that led to the diagnosis of anorexia nervosa as panhypopituitarism (a malfunction of the pituitary gland

that can lead to loss of appetite). Simmonds' findings shifted the emphasis from a psychological to a physical cause, and for the next twenty years doctors held by a single-cause explanation for all adolescent emaciation.

By the 1930s several physicians began to question the physiological origin of anorexia nervosa. Research in the late 1940s demonstrated conclusively that "developmental traumas and interferences, as well as psychosocial stress, can alter hormone patterns and secretions..." (Sours, p. 40). These research results provided an increased interest in the psychobiology of anorexia nervosa.

Between the late 1930s and 1960, researchers depended primarily on the psychoanalytic approach to explain and treat anorexia nervosa. Older psychoanalytic concepts have leaned "heavily on theories about fixation at the oral level of psychosexual development, or regression of instinctual drives from the genital level of development, and on symptom formation around oral conflicts" (Ross, 1977, p. 424; Jessner and Abse, 1960; Moulton, 1942; Thomas, 1967; Waller, Kaufman, and Deutsch, 1940).

The latest phase in the theory and diagnosis of anorexia developed over the period from 1960 to 1982. Katz (1982, in press) conducted research that shows a link between anorexia nervosa and abnormal function of the hypothalamus, but he does not suggest abnormal functions of the master gland as a cause of the disorder. Indeed, it is possible that a starvation diet may be a factor in disturbing hypothalmic function.

Katz has been joined in research on hypothalamic misfunction by several others, including Boyar *et al.* (1976), Russell (1965), Dally (1969), and Halmi *et al.* (1978). These researchers have found no demonstrable pituitary dysfunction in anorexia nervosa, thus further repudiating Simmonds' earlier theory.

Psychoanalytic causation theories from 1960 on have stressed the maladaptive efforts of the anorexic to establish self-identity apart from the mother. Selvini-Palazzoli (1974) sees at the core of anorexia nervosa the anorexic's perception of her body as a threatening entity whose growth must be stopped. Selvini-Palazzoli depicts the typical anorexic's mother as overprotective, unable to see her daughter as a separate entity. She controls her child, thwarting efforts to derive pleasure separate from herself. When the child complies, she is rewarded. The young girl begins to feel unable to learn apart from her mother's signals, a process which contributes to the daughter's ego-depression. At puberty the girl experiences a split between the incorporating ego and the identifying ego: that is, between the body and the sense of self. The body, according to Selvini-Palazzoli's theory, becomes invested with primitive and negative identifications. It becomes symbolically equated with severe discontent with self.

Bruch (1970, 1973a, 1979) has developed a theory of anorexia which emphasizes the psychoanalytic libido less but instead uses explanations derived from neurophysiology and neuropsychology. Bruch speaks of falsified learning experiences: incorrect learning experiences acquired during different maturational levels and codified neurologically. In her developmental theory, Bruch starts with a sequence of presymbolic concepts, borrowing from the Swiss psychologist Piaget. Unless the mother teaches a child to recognize hunger as a distinct and separate need, the child fails to respond specifically and appropriately to internal signals of nutritional need. Thus Bruch contends that one's perception of hunger and appetite is largely a matter of learning.

Furthermore, Bruch contends that the anorexic manifests a delusional distortion of body image. The anorexic denies emaciation while maintaining a fear of ugliness and obesity. The anorexic also experiences disturbances in interpretation of body stimuli, including denial of the stimuli that trigger recognition of hunger and appetite, fatigue, weakness, and cold. Sexual feelings may also go unrecognized; emotional states may not evoke appropriate responses. The anorexic experiences herself as ineffective, a state Bruch relates developmentally to the other disturbances. Defiance and negativism arise alongside the sense of ineffectiveness. For Bruch the key to anorexia nervosa is the need for autonomy and a sense of effectiveness, maladaptively sought through control over the body.

Regardless of the school of interpretation to which one subscribes in order to understand anorexia nervosa, the syndrome presents one of the most frustrating maladies seen by clinicians.

No researcher disputes the increasing frequency of this illness. While estimates of affected numbers vary, one can assume that any family with a female child has a chance as high as 1-in-100 to be affected directly by anorexia nervosa.

A variety of factors may play a role in a particular individual's predisposition toward anorexia nervosa. Weiner (1977) and Kubie (1971) wrote descriptions of illness models important in the understanding of anorexia nervosa. Weiner suggests that multiple events predispose a person to anorexia, even though the illness occurs at a particular time. As the individual fails to adapt to specific internal and external demands the illness develops. Kubie, on the other hand, believes that illness is a process and that anorexia is caused by the continuous interaction between the individual, her symptoms, and her environment, even as she strives to overcome her symptoms.

However, even if particular characteristics predispose one toward an illness, not everyone will develop that illness; nor will everyone with a particular illness have all the predisposing factors. All illnesses are heterogeneous, and so is anorexia nervosa. In a summary of a model of any illness Weiner (1977) has said:

1) illness often results from an interplay of predisposing forces acting upon an individual;
2) of many people with the predisposition to an illness, only some actually develop it;
3) for individuals with a disease the exact interaction of predisposing forces will vary; and
4) the same predisposing factors may actually develop in ferent people in different ways.

Weiner continues that the onset of illness is determined by the failure of the individual to adapt to a variety of demands put to her. Furthermore, the predisposing events that determine *what type* of illness will result may be quite different from the events that determine *when* the individual becomes ill. Finally, the circumstances which perpetuate the disorder may either predispose one to illness or initiate a case (Weiner, 1977, p. 13).

If one follows the model of Kubie, one views illness as an ongoing process. It emanates from the interactions between an individual and the external world, between symptoms and the attempts to deal with those symptoms, and the resulting experience of the illness itself. When an individual attempts to deal with an illness, behavior and personality changes can sometimes account for symptoms that later perpetuate the disorder.

For the best understanding of anorexia nervosa, all possible factors ought to be considered in each particular case. It is necessary to review factors within the individual, her family, and her culture to see what might predispose her to the ailment. It is necessary to investigate possible initiating or precipitating factors in her life. And it is important to consider how her physical symptoms might actually be sustaining and elaborating her illness (Garfinkel and Garner, 1982).

Bruch (1973b) and Selvini-Palazzoli (1974) stressed the anorexic's feeling of ineffectiveness, her inability to function separately from a strong family member or other influential person. The anorexic experiences a deficit in autonomy and self-mastery of her own body. She believes she is not in control of her needs and impulses; she fears she does not have possession of her own body; and she does not retain within herself her own center of gravity. On the contrary, the anorexic feels that external forces exert the most influence on her life. She becomes a product of others' thoughts and actions. So long as the potential anorexic remains in a protected situation or environment, she may retain feelings of security sufficient to prevent the onset of anorexia. But a change in environment or change in demands may be enough to initiate anorexia.

Adolescence is a time of many changes, and it is also the time that anorexia typically shows up. Crisp (1980) discusses the frustrations of forming one's own identity during adolescence, when dependency needs are still strong. "An individual's sense of self and worth in our society is, partly at least, a socially and psychologically based phenomenon, and becomes established in relation to the social and cultural context, initially provided by the family and its value systems, beliefs and capacity to share and nurture" (p. 56). The process of identity formation occurs over several years and requires "the integration of the new biological sexuality within oneself both with one's basic social needs, sense of self-esteem and competence and one's set of values" (p. 57).

Upheaval always follows the process of identity formation, because new ideas and values must be tested, sometimes at the expense of values and attitudes held by the family. Feelings of anger and guilt, resulting in depression, are common during these adolescent years. For many the adjustment succeeds, and the individual becomes a stable adult with a strong sense of identity. But others do not adjust to the task of identity formation and for them, the demands may bring on emotional trauma and illness.

Emerging sexuality complicates the adolescent's task with both biological and social demands. But sexual identity begins way back in childhood, when basic gender expectations arise. If confusion or ambivalence in this area develops in early childhood, all the more reason for maturational difficulties in adolescence.

Adolescent changes in the body may give rise to new concerns. Crisp (1970) feels that the anorexic's "weight phobia" comes from a desperate attempt to avoid the normal body proportions that accompany maturation. Some anorexics have been found to experience early puberty, suggesting that they lacked the psychological maturity to deal with the demands of biological development.

Strober (in press), trying to study the anorexic personality, compared twenty-two 12- to 16-year-old anorexic females with patients of the same age experiencing other affective or personality disorders. None of the anorexic patients had been ill as long as a year, so no chronic effects would skew the study. Both groups took standard psychological tests in unison. On the Marlowe-Crowne Social Desirability Scale, the anorexics scored significantly higher, confirming the notion that they need approval from others. The California Psychological Inventory revealed the anorexic patients' tendencies toward conformity, conscientiousness, and lack of responsiveness to inner needs.

Sours (1980) reports that runners and anorexics have much in common. Each seeks to dominate, perfect, and control the body; each is driven to experience self-esteem derived through some particular agony. Sours concludes, "Running, like fasting and starvation, narrows the distance between what the runner is and what

he can be, between the ideal self and the actual self, between as-
piration and reality" (p. 280). But despite the anorexic's efforts,
childhood feelings of worthlessness and inadequacy remain, demanding forever more appeasement.

Feelings of inadequacy and low personal worth may serve as
predisposing factors to anorexia nervosa. These feelings make one
look to others, especially the family, for personal values, even for
a sense of one's own self. Separating from the parent, although
one would presume that it would promote strength and independence, may actually bring on anorexia in a person already predisposed to the disorder.

Family and Cultural Aspects of Anorexia Nervosa

Some researchers, like Sours (1980), take a psychoanalytic approach to the question of how family influences affect the anorexic
personality. But other research findings emphasize other patterns
of cause and effect in family interactions.

Menuchin *et al.* (1975) suggested that most anorexics grow up
in psychosomatic families. The typical anorexic's household tends
to be "overprotected, painfully sensitive to conflict, and rigidly
determined to maintain the status quo" (quoted in Sours, 1980)—
in other words, an environment of inflexibility in contrast to the
"normal" family environment in western culture, which en-
courages separation, individuation, and autonomy while still providing protection and security. In the typical family, each member plays a role within understood boundaries, an arrangement
that permits arguments, discussions, and even some forms of ag-
gression in response to internal and external family change. As a
child matures, her role changes. She becomes less enmeshed in
family interactions, more disengaged to lead her own life. In
short, flexibility allows the opportunity for growth to occur. Conflict can be resolved without sacrificing autonomy.

But in the anorexic family, distress and conflicts are hidden
vigilantly. The child is protected from herself, so much so that
even her body is not her own. Living in such a protective environment, the anorexic's coping and defense mechanisms are

minimized and held to an infantile level. When her behavior shows signs of growing up, she may often be viewed as disloyal and destructive to her family. She becomes hypersensitive to herself, intolerant of any failures she perceives in her character, convinced of her own incompetence, and unable to engage in realistic self-evaluation. She defends against family enmeshment through denial, negativism, and the pursuit of perfection.

Anorexics usually grow up in middle-upper or upper-class families (Bruch, 1973; Crisp *et al.* 1974), which usually means that the anorexic has grown up with higher IQ, body concern, health food awareness, early menarche, and aversion to carbohydrates. Most of these families are comfortably well off, but often they still envy affluent friends and neighbors, believing that affluence represents perfection attained. Jealousy and rivalry exist among siblings and parents. In a family where professional goals are valued, demands and expectations are high. Often mothers in these households engage in work primarily for self-actualization, rather than because the family needs a second income.

Crisp *et al.* (1977a) found that when anorexia nervosa occurs in the lower social classes, the psychopathology is more severe. The disease is atypical in this social context, and the anorexic from this background frequently feels heightened anxiety in sexual relationships, often as a result of rape or other aggressive sexual experiences.

Many researchers (Bruch, 1971, 1978, 1979, and others) have discovered that frequently the anorexic is convinced that she comes from the perfect family where there are no conflicts, no tensions, and no disharmony. Parents themselves often point to the anorexic as a model child, usually exemplary in every way. She is the offspring who never caused any trouble, who never disobeyed or expressed dissatisfaction. When a daughter must resort to anorexia to express feelings of rebellion and suffering, the illness begins to disrupt the parents' lives seriously. Somehow they have failed to transmit to the child a feeling of her value and self-worth, and she is reacting through her willful refusal to eat.

Typically, the anorexic child has grown up in a household where she was cared for physically, educationally, and materially.

But somewhere along the way toward maturity, her concepts of body and bodily functions have become confused, as well as her sense of identity, autonomy, and self-control. She misperceives or misinterprets body sensations. Bruch believes that she never properly learned the signals for hunger awareness. A child may even find it difficult to determine whether a sensation originates inside or out.

Feeding histories are investigated during the course of an anorexic's therapy, but often the findings are colorless. The mother reports that she never permitted the child to be hungry or that the child was compliant and undemanding, eating whatever was set before her.

Some parents—and particularly in British families, governesses—may demand that the child always clean her plate without consideration to preferences, aversions, or serving size. A dutifully obedient child complies, but never gets the opportunity to practice self-regulation in eating. Years later this same child may doubt her ability to stop at or before satiety on her own.

Anorexics, predisposed to dichotomous thinking, tend to evaluate their parents as all-good and all-wise. When shortcomings in her mother (or father) come to view, the anorexic may panic, believing that by discovering parental fault she is risking complete rejection, anger, and vulnerability.

Stemming from her low sense of self-esteem, the anorexic may have trouble accepting gifts. She may feel she does not deserve them, she may not know what she wants, and she may not understand how to express her uncertainty. Sometimes she will anticipate a coming gift and rehearse enthusiasm for it, despite not really wanting it. Rather than risk disappointing the parent giving her a gift, the anorexic girl dutifully will express unfelt enthusiasm. At least one patient on the record confessed total confusion when asked to make a list of things she might like. That sort of independent decision was alien to her, so unable was she to distinguish between what she wanted and what her parents wanted for her in matters both large and small.

Anorexics lack self-assertion. They over-exemplify submissiveness and pay abnormal consideration to the judgments of others.

Without a sense of their own autonomy, they do not make decisions because they do not trust their own opinions and judgment. They learned their conditioning early. They learned what others wanted them to do and say. They stay bound to those values and convictions of earlier periods, even when circumstances urge them on.

Despite academic excellence and high I.Q.'s—commonly 120 and above (Dally and Gomez, 1979)—the emotional development of anorexics seems to get stuck at a level of very basic, child-like operations. Most adolescents learn to use formal operations in their personal relations, but Bruch (1973, 1979) found those skills devoid or deficient in anorexics.

Parents tend to remain unaware of the way their children interpret words or actions literally. Chance remarks can be incorrectly processed and stored in the memories of hypersensitive kids. Anorexics are sensitive to negative comments from parents. They do not tolerate peer teasing or criticism well. They go so far as to imagine random comments to be insults. Exaggerated concern for the reactions of others makes decisions difficult for anorexics. Any event that fosters anxiety can trigger the onset of anorexia, even though that event was just a catalysst and not a causal factor on its own. Clearly, a potential anorexic personality can get herself tied up in knots. The girl becomes vulnerable to dissatisfaction with herself. She feels her failure so painfully that she is likely to blame her body for the distress. She attempts to alleviate it by changing her relationship with her mother and her body—a misguided search for control and mastery by self-starvation.

An anorexic lives in constant fear of being unloved or rejected by her family or teachers. Friendships generally do not last long because she fearfully holds back from contributing to the relationship. Believing herself incapable of an identity as an individual, chameleon-like she adopts the personality or opinions of those around her. She constantly tests herself against others in her mind to determine whether someone else has a better student record or a thinner figure. She never wins in her comparisons, and she doubts she could ever compete equally.

Sours (1980), Garfinkel and Garner (1982), and Bruch (1973, 1979), among others, have investigated ethnic links with anorexia nervosa. The findings do not link the illness with any particular group, although its incidence seems to be more common "in subcultures where food, eating, and family solidarity, especially at the dining room table, are important . . . the disturbance is widely found in 'WASPdom'" (Sours, p. 274). Where food is plentiful, anorexia follows.

In a nation of plenty, the adolescent considers eating what one wants an adult privilege. The normal adolescent may voice preferences outspokenly, demanding or refusing certain foods. Food fads are common at this age, but most adolescents seem to know what they want and how much they want of it. Sensing those needs and acting upon them is part of the adult self-regulating mechanism that develops in harmony with the body's physiological requirements.

However, in the obese and the starving adolescent, the self-regulating mechanism appears to be "grossly disturbed," not because of an organic defect but because awareness of physiological needs is lacking. A young person unaware of bodily sensations cannot exert control over the functions normally associated with those sensations. Anorexic adherence to a voluntary starvation regimen suggests some inability in recognizing the symptoms accompanying hunger. The anorexic ignores the secondary signals of listlessness and fatigue as well. Indeed, despite inward signs of extreme hunger, outwardly the anorexic may appear proud and cheerful, even hyperactive.

Bruch agrees that the idea that hunger is a learned experience may sound outlandish; yet she cites Hebb (1949) to demonstrate that eating behavior contains important learned features. Even in rats appropriate food-seeking behavior must be acquired, so that cognitive factors must enter into the study of "hunger" and "satiation." These observations call into question the concept of hunger as an innate drive. Their psychoanalytic ramifications belong within a context larger than this study; but for the understanding of anorexia nervosa, early lessons about eating must play an important role, considering how frequently food is deliberately accepted or rejected—as in obesity or anorexia nervosa—as a way of expressing or combating anxiety, or as a way of handling intra-psychic and interpersonal tensions.

"Abnormal eating habits do not occur in isolation but are always associated with other difficulties in the area of active or passive self-awareness and in the sense of identity," as Bruch states (1973, p. 186). From birth on, two basic forms of behavior must be differentiated: infant-initiated behavior, on the one hand; behavior in response to outside stimuli on the other. These distinctions hold true in the infant's social-emotional field of experience as well as in the infant's biological stratum. A child either initiates behavior or she responds to stimuli, from inside or out. It is also important to evaluate whether the interaction between the infant and its environment is appropriate—that is, whether the interaction serves the infant's survival and development or impedes that development.

If the child responds appropriately to signals from within her body, her diffuse urges become organized in such a way that self-awareness and effectiveness develop. But if the child's efforts do not receive steady and consistent confirmation, then a child develops amidst perplexity and disturbances in her body or her world. Patterns of interaction observed in the homes of obese and anorexic patients demonstrated "Glaring disregard for a young patient's individuality and expressed needs or discomfort..." (Bruch, 1973, p. 187).

As long as a child remains in the environment where mother's demands parallel the child's physiological needs, a façade of normality may result, with no hint of anorexia appearing. But when the child encounters the demands of new situations, for which the routines of her early life have left her unprepared, she begins to reveal gross deficits in initiative, inner controls, and active self-expression. Without an integrated body concept, she will feel helpless in response to growing bodily urges or inability to cope with the psychological and social demands of adolescence.

Abnormal eating patterns and body size are the obvious symptoms of anorexia, but developmental deficits are often present in other arenas of the anorexic girl's life. Many an anorexic is described by her parent as having been obedient and compliant. She never participated in rough behavior, she never exhibited impudence toward her elders, she never carried in other mischievous activities that characterize most childhoods. Why these problems now? Without engaging in these normal childhood activities that let a youngster work through some rebellious feelings the pressure builds inside. The venting in an anorexic comes through self-starvation and inner-directed anger.

Several studies have documented the importance of early transactions between mother and child, essential in aiding the child to perceive and differentiate her own needs from those ascribed to her by others (Escalona, 1953; Piaget, 1953; and Spitz, 1965).

Investigations of the psychological causes behind anorexia nervosa certainly yield no absolute answers, but they do offer clues important for parents as to the factors that can inhibit the normal individuation of the infant and child.

Socio-cultural influences outside the home certainly cannot be denied. The body of research on anorexia often alludes to cultural influences but does not quantify the *extent* of the influence of media or cultural dictates on eating disorders.

"In our society, control of food becomes an important feature in defining class," says Dr. Arnold Anderson, from the Johns Hopkins School of Medicine (*U.S. News and World Report*, Aug. 30, 1982, p. 47). He cites studies showing that more than 70 percent of women in Western cultures believe that they are overweight. Anderson imputes part of this attitude to the current fashion magazines that idealize the gaunt female form.

The same magazine quotes Dr. Craig Johnson, director of the eating disorder project, Michael Reese Hospital in Chicago; Dr. Richard MacKenzie, chief of adolescent medicine, Los Angeles Children's Hospital; and Dr. Joel Yager director of the eating disorder clinic, UCLA, among other authorities on eating disorders. Johnson found that women pictured in magazine centerfolds today are significantly thinner than they were 20 years ago. Miss America winners have averaged 10 percent thinner than other contestants in the last several years. "Thin is in," and the movement appears to have increased impact on the females of the nation.

Sours (*Science Digest*, July 1981, p. 56) mentions three other cultural components of anorexia nervosa today. He points out that women are under increasing pressure to compete with men. To the troubled individual, starvation appears as a method of sharpening competitive skills and exerting power. He further points out that as child-rearing practices change, children of affluent families may be pushed more rapidly into adulthood. In a world where both adults and children have lost faith in the institutions of government and religion, a sense of powerlessness, of being overwhelmed, can easily develop. Finally, Sours believes that political warnings that the world is exhausting its resources are making anorexia the appropriate disorder for the coming Era of Depletion: "Not hunger but its opposite, overeating, is feared by Western culture."

In the same vein Sours elsewhere (1980) suggests broader societal and cultural explanations for the increased incidence of anorexia nervosa. Shallow relationships, vulnerable to exploitation, engender insecurity, as do narcissistic therapies which have replaced religion with the celebration of the self. Parents, skeptical about their own and society's future, ignore the needs of their children and comfort themselves in soon-dissolved marriages. Such events "blur the boundaries of the self, make people feel vulnerable to passivity, loss of control, and liable to intrusion, invasion, and control by vague, outside forces. Anorectics dread obliteration by the outside world—a world represented by food" (p.283).

Despite the effects of society, Sours, as others, concludes that childhood traumas and impaired object relations are still a major factor in anorexia. "Attempts at the realization of the 'perfect image' is one 'solution' for the anorectic, the runner, and many other individuals in our society, to childhood feelings of worthlessness and inadequacy. . . . Perfection is no cure for pain—for either the runner, the anorectic, or anybody else. Narcissistic restitutive efforts are maladaptive; they do not correct distortions in the sense of physical and mental well being, when distorting defects occurred early in the formation of the self" (p. 286).

Clinical Manifestation and Treatment

Researchers have identified two types of anorexia: primary cases in which the illness is the self-contained cluster of symptoms already evoked in this book; and secondary cases in which the symptomatology involves refusal to eat but for reasons other than fear of fat. A person with certain mental disorders may refuse to eat because of fear that food is poisoned: an example of secondary anorexia. But for the purposes of this study, only primary anorexia is considered.

Feighner *et al.* (1972) developed the description widely accepted in diagnosing anorexia nervosa. The following criteria must be found *together* for an accurate diagnosis as anorexia.

1. The patient must be under age 25 at onset of the illness. The typical patient is a girl just past puberty. Although males also develop anorexia nervosa, only 1 in 15 cases is male (Crisp and Toms, 1972), with onset frequently prepubertal (Bruch, 1973).

2. The patient must show a weight loss of at least 25 percent of original body weight or, in adolescents, a weight 25 percent below accepted standards for age and height. In some individuals, clearly a sound weight-reduction diet in response to actual obesity or self-consciousness about being fat, may result in such losses but not constitute anorexia, making it initially difficult for the physician to detect where the diet ends and the disease begins.

3. The patient has no illness that can account for the weight loss.

4. The patient holds "a distorted, implacable attitude towards eating, food, or weight that overrides hunger, admonitions, reassurance, and threats" (Feiner, *et al.* p. 57). In their unending quest for thinness, patients may exhibit distorted attitudes in a number of ways: denial of illness despite emaciation; manipulating or deceiving medical personnel and family members, who insist they eat; obtaining overt pleasure from food refusal and weight loss; expressing distorted judgments of nutritional needs and intake; and/or developing unusual patterns of food handling, like hoarding or cooking excessively for others.

5. The patient has no other psychiatric disorder. Psychological

profiles, such as the Minnesota Multiphasic Personality Inventory (MMPI), generally test out normal. And yet the anorexic is often a perfectionist, highly eager to please, an overachiever, and a victim of distorted body imagery. Primary affective disorders, schizophrenia, and obsessive-compulsive or phobic neuroses are not present.

Other physical signs and symptoms accompany the foregoing major critera. Feighner *et al.* require *at least two* of the following additional symptoms to warrant a diagnosis of anorexia nervosa: amenorrhea (absence of menstrual periods), lanugo (a fine hair covering on the face, chest, or back), bradycardia (persistent resting pulse of less than 60 beats per minute), periodic overactivity, episodic bulimia (overeating), and self-induced vomiting. Recent information suggests that no upper age limit can be set. Patients over 40 have sought treatment, although onset may have preceded this age by several years.

The biology of human starvation has been recorded by several researchers in studies undertaken on released prisoners-of-war and voluntary subjects (Silverstone 1975, Brozek, Wills and Keys 1946, and Keys and associates 1950). The clinical manifestations of actual starvation also apply to victims of anorexia nervosa. In general, starvation leads to apathy, fatigue, mental depression, withdrawal, loss of libido, and preoccupation with food that can translate into dreams and fantasies about food and eating. Hunger continues, even up until the time of death by starvation.

A starving individual may participate in theft or violence; shoplifting of food, especially in bulimics, is not uncommon. Human feelings tend to become coarser during starvation, alongside concomitant indifference to the needs and emotions of others. Irritability, labile moods, and occasional lapses into psychotic states of confusion can accompany starvation. Even trivial decisions become difficult when drive and spontaneity are lost through lack of food. The starving organism becomes sluggish, weak, deeply depressed, and lethargic. These symptoms increase with the duration and intensity of food deprivation.

Anorexics often flirt with these life-threatening characteristics of starvation. The anorexic is ever hungry, but she tries to displace her hunger by engaging in behaviors like persistently feeding others, drinking large quantities of non-nutritional fluids such as diet colas, binge-purging, or exercising frenetically. Many anorexics deny their hunger during the day only to experience it acutely in the night. Bulimics often lose control during the night, too, and indulge in gorging behavior. Anorexics have been known to continue starvation for months or years, after which their stomach becomes atonic and contracted (Crisp, 1967). These changes in the digestive system do not affect hunger, except that the duration and quantity of food held in the system are reduced. Then the anorexic complains of the sensations of "bloating" and "fullness," which she uses as an excuse not to eat.

The anorexic physiology shows marked signs of the starvation regimen. She becomes cadaverous. She experiences extreme intolerance to cold because of hypothermia and loss of insulating fat stores. She may contract edema. Her skin texture changes to a sandpapery, yellowed condition, often covered with long, silky lanugo hair that my appear on the trunk, extemities, and back. Occasionally the skin of a bulimic is hot, clammy, and flushed from eating binges. Severe dehydration from induced diarrhea may prove life-threatening. Scalp hair may thin but baldness does not occur. There can be a high incidence of dental caries and gingival deterioration. Hands and feet may become cyanotic, nails by become brittle. In short, an anorexic resembles an inmate from a concentration camp.

Suidice attempts rarely characterize anorexia. Dally and Gomez (1979), Russell (1979), and others have discussed suicide attempts among their cases. Most attempts involved wrist-slashing or drug overdoses, but they were primarily atypical cases, often older patients, or those who binge and become deeply depressed. The typical anorexic depends so much on omnipotence from beyond that her own death seems impossible.

Deaths from anorexia nervosa have been reported. Studies cited figures anywhere from 1 to 10 percent (Sours, 1968; Crisp, 1969; Asbeck *et al.*, 1972). The anorexic herself rarely realizes the extent of physical danger, rarely considers the possibility of death, even when death is imminent. When death occurs in the anorexic, it usually results from a metabolic electrolyte disturbance that precipitates cardiac arrest.

Now that eating disorders have been identified and anorexia nervosa singled out as a separate syndrome, work on effective treatments is underway. But as the causes for this ailment are mixed, so are treatment possibilities and practices. Specific treatments range "from traditional psychoanalysis to psycho-surgery, from education to behavioral modification, from simple observation and therapeutic indifference—allowing the natural history to run its course—to an intense family treatment" (Sours, 1980).

Pharmacotherapy, intravenous feeding, insulin therapy, electro-convulsive shock, and other extreme treatments are still used to some extent. But most practitioners agree that these sorts of remedies are counterproductive, since they lead the anorexic away from the psychological underpinnings of her disorder.

Any early form of treatment will try to restore nutrition to prevent further starvation and to mitigate the mental effects of starvation. The question of whether hospitalization helps is debatable (Minuchin et al., 1978; Browning and Miller, 1968). But when the body weight goes as low as 60 pounds, medical confinement may be the only alternative.

When hospitalization is necesary, the patient should be admitted to a medical unit that has personnel who are knowledgable in the pathology of anorexia nervosa (Pierloot, Wellens, and Houben, 1976; Moldofsky and Garfinkel, 1974). The medical doctor, therapist, nursing staff, and others involved with the patient must work together, using treatment practices upon which they have agreed. The better they understand the ailment and the treatment they are applying to it, the better they will work together toward a healthy recovery.

Once the anorexic's life is no longer threatened, long-term psychological treatment begins, treatment that rarely continues as long as it should. In some instances the patient terminates treatment or the family withdraws support of it. In other circumstances the therapist, seeing nutrition restored, may end treatment. But rarely is the patient ready to return to normal life at this point, confident in her ability to cope. If she returns to a family situation still crippled with impaired interactions, the prognosis for long-term improvement is not good.

Schools of thought differ concerning the more effective sex of the therapist in anorexia. The point is crucial in establishing the necessary rapport between therapist and client, but perhaps a trusting relationship is more important in treatment than any methodology. Selvini-Palazzoli (1974) advocates a female therapist with whom the patient can develop a "symbolic erotic bond," which may help the girl detach from the mother and accept heterosexuality. The female therapist can also serve as a role-model for womanhood with which the girl can identify. Some researchers recommend a male therapist as the strong, caring father figure the anorexic may need. Szyrynski (1973) avers that it is positively reinforcing to a girl to realize that she can attract a man and gain pleasure from his attention. Furthermore, he contends that a male therapist may replace an inadequate father-figure and will escape any identification with a hostile mother. No conclusive evidence points toward one sex as preferable over the other in selecting a therapist to treat anorexia. Again, the individual needs of each particular patient are the paramount factors by which the decision ought to be made.

The therapist does not have to be trained in medicine, although medical training may be helpful. A practitioner is less prone to panic at the physical fluctuations of the anorexic, but anyone experienced in the treatment of this disorder will be aware of the course it might take. A close alliance must exist between the therapist and medical support personnel to monitor the physical condition of the patient.

Flexibility in the therapist helps, because then the therapy can change in response to new information gained. It also reassures the anorexic, usually very rigid in behavior, that she can trust someone flexible, which can provide a useful model. Patients need to be relieved of the anxeity of abandonment after they meet their desired weight goals. As they go deeper into therapy and realize the extent of the underlying problems, anorexics may become overwhelmed, assuming that without a weight problem they have no value or interest to the therapist. Therefore their logic demands that they hold on to their eating symptoms to legitimize continued treatment. The therapist can allay these fears by discussing the course of treatment, with guarantees that it will continue as long as necessary, not just until the scales hit a certain number.

Many practitioners recognize the need to convey to the anorexic that the therapist understands the processes of the disorder, that what appears bizarre and frightening is not unique to this person, and that the therapist is experienced in treating the syndrome.

It may seem contradictory to advocate forming a strong support bond between therapist and client when dependence has been a problem in the anorexic's life to this point. But this bond contributes to future progress rather than hindering her. She establishes a trusting relationship that permits her to work through her own underlying problems, achieve self-understanding, and thus establish the delayed independence.

Many an anorexic is reluctant to enter into a relationship with anyone, let alone a physician or therapist who may be perceived as an agent to rob her of control. For some time the anorexic will view treatment solely as a way to make her eat and get fat. Because previously the patient has felt inferior, insignificant, or subjugated by others, she will not initially see the therapeutic setting any differently. Thus it becomes essential for the therapist to establish an atmosphere of privacy and openness, to reassure the client who will be quick to seek suspicious motives.

Treatment often begins differently in the case of anorexia nervosa as compared to other psychological disorders. Whereas in other disorders the patient seeks out the help, admitting something is awry, the anorexic begins treatment at the urging of someone else. She may be uncooperative, negativistic, or defiant. The family perceives the need for therapy intervention before the patient does. If they do not act they are at fault; if they do take measures the patient resents them. Obviously the therapy has to take into consideration family involvement at some point in its course.

The patient needs to realize that therapy is not exclusively for weight gain and that her diet is only one aspect of the total picture. She may be reassured to learn that some bizarre symptoms may in part be physiologically motivated and not exclusively psychological, brought on by starvation itself. This realization may allay some anxiety over being emotionally out of control.

Double forces interact to keep the anorexic grasping tight to her symptoms. One of these drives is a fear of fatness; the other is a drive for thinness (Bruch, 1973). She feels positively reinforced for increasing thinness, on both counts. Continued weight loss is the answer to the fear of fatness and it also offers visible results as gratification for limiting intake. Furthermore, the anorexic does not *want* to lose her anxiety over food and fear of weight gain. What to others are averse experiences—hunger and deprivation—function for her as the signal that she is successfully maintaining the higher-order virtue of low weight. The treadmill continuously turns.

Encouraging an anorexic to examine currently held values and to liberate herself from punishingly high standards are cornerstones in the treatment of anorexia nervosa. Other guidelines for the therapeutic treatment of anorexia appeared in the winter 1981 issue of "International Journal of Eating Disorders."

One of the major goals of psychotherapy in the treatment of anorexia nervosa is to assist victims in correcting their distorted sense of reality. The patients apply faulty thinking and beliefs to the world around them as well as to themselves. This realignment of thought processes must occur gradually and carefully so that the anorexic really believes in her new views and perceptions *at this point*. At the same time misconceptions and erroneous thinking must be identified as such during therapy, with the therapist actually explaining faulty thinking to the patient.

Beck (1978) has identified some types of logical errors in the thinking of depressives and phobics. Anorexics may commit a number of these same types of errors, along with others. Three of the most common reasoning errors displayed by anorexic patients are dichotomous thinking, personalization, and superstitious thinking.

Anorexics customarily exhibit the all-or-nothing characteristics of dichotomous thinking, and this absolutist frame of mind applies to many areas of her life besides weight. Career, studies, sports all receive her rigidly addressed behavior. She tends to believe that she must maintain self-control, independence, conflict avoidance, social approval, and self-confidence completely and continuously. The anorexic is apprehensive of unstructured time and of the future, because it cannot be predicted and controlled. She fears the inability to cope with the consequences of potentially unpredictable events, so she attempts to establish rigid control through compulsive rules and obsessional or superstitious thinking.

Therapy can help the anorexic realize that she can cope amidst change, without catastrophic results. Typically her first response to such freedom will be a shift from overcompliance to stubbornness, typical of dichotomous thinking. But gradually she will become aware that life need not be lived in all-or-nothing fashion.

Personalization and self-reference is another behavior pattern frequently observed in anorexics, a manifestation which in itself is almost a dichotomy as well. In personalization, she holds the egocentric belief that she is center-stage in attention. While this may be true in an enmeshed family situation, it is clearly not true in many other situations. But the anorexic has trouble distinguishing when it is and when it is not true. Ironically, she considers herself an important object, but from that attention she infers disapproval from others. "*They* won't think I'm skinny," she thinks, in believing that all strangers notice her weight. "*They* think I'm not successful...."

The anorexic must be trained in "decentering," a process whereby personalization and self-reference are discouraged. The patient learns in therapy to realize how rarely she attends to others with the intensity she imagines in others' awareness of her. By looking at her standards of judging others she learns that she judges others far less harshly than she does herself, and realizes that others see her less harshly also. Decentering is a time-consuming process of restructuring values and perception, but small improvements mean a lot. A person who tends to personalize can prove resistant to change, but improvements are possible.

Anorexics also engage in superstitious thinking, the sort of illogical thought that occurs when the patient sees a cause-effect relationship between two actually unrelated events. The anorexic often establishes elaborate rituals to stave off some imagined ill effects, supposed to minimize or forestall some threatening consequence. Superstitious thinking is deeply engrained in anorexics. In fact, according to Bandura (1978), "avoidance behavior is so powerfully controlled by bizarre internal contingencies that neither the beliefs nor the accompanying actions are much affected even by extremely punishing environmental consequences" (p. 351). Rationally the anorexic realizes the fallacy of this sort of reasoning, but still she persists in superstitious thinking. Correction occurs by encouraging true tests of these thoughts up against reality. After lengthy process, superstitious thinking can diminish.

Therapy must also work to eradicate faulty assumptions that often form the framework for specific attitudes. Several such assumptions are prominent in the thinking of the anorexic. One, of course, is the assumption that weight is the sole determinant of self-worth. Anorexics also assume that complete self-control and discipline are essential; that perfect performance is necessary for self-fulfillment; that one must always meet others' expectations; and that parents are beyond criticism. The anorexic clings tenaciously to these beliefs and must be divested of them slowly and carefully. In therapy the clinician may help alleviate the hold by articulating the assumptions, a process that can defuse the impact. Also, the patient can be led through a generalized application of the assumptions to test their validity when measuring others besides herself.

Bruch (1977) cautions against a psychoanalytic approach that interprets her feelings for the anorexic. This approach only reinforces the engrained belief that she does not know her own feelings. At a pivotal point of treatment, the therapist can help the patient discover how she truly feels and how to develop a sense of genuineness about her own emotions. Incongruous expressions of feeling in early therapy result from the patient responding according to what she thinks she *should* feel. The sufferer must be guided away from reliance on her expectations of others' reactions, toward realizing her own reactions and emotions.

One exception to the goal of helping the anorexic discover her own beliefs and feelings lies in the area of her distorted concept of body shape. "A healthy mind in a healthy body," as the classical saying puts it. Health cannot be established until the body is perceived correctly, but those very perceptions must arise from a body recovering from extreme strain. But the anorexic's therapist still has to help the anorexic see herself. Gradually, the subjective interpretation of body shape gives way to understanding. The patient is encouraged to marshal all her arguments in the process, so that they may be tested against reality. Most authorities agree that prognosis quickly improves once distortions in body image fade.

The anorexic has never learned to trust the accuracy of her own thoughts, feelings, or perceptions. If one cannot believe in internally derived conclusions, then one must depend heavily upon external criteria. The human organism, with its adaptive ability, creates ways to compensate for deficits. The anorexic adapts through extreme self-discipline and the need to control herself at all times. Therapy works to break this pattern of maladaptive behavior.

Reading about the symptoms and psychology of anorexia nervosa still doesn't evoke for a non-member of the anorexic sorority the sense of utter terror in loss of control. Feelings of despair and worthlessness are appeased only when the scale affirms more weight loss or when the body accepts the challenge of still more kinetic activity. It is as if all the forces of one's being, all the consuming self-hatred and disorientation, are fused into a deadly laser beam at the dial of a bathroom scale. Losing pounds represents an anorexic's maturation, her cognition, and her passion. And unless the therapist and the family realize the anorexic's intensity, I do not foresee success.

Be very careful in extinguishing anorexic behavior because even if only a whispery ember remains, it may flare up again. The anorexic fears total extinction of her behavior patterns. Destroy her *raison d'être* and there is nothing left. The only way out of this fear is to replace distortion with reality, but it must be done carefully, patiently, non-threateningly.

The therapeutic steps outlined above take a more cognitive and affective than psychoanalytic tack.

On the other hand, some clinicians disavow the anorexic's need for therapy, believing that good nursing is sufficient or that only crisis intervention is called for. Their theory is that left to itself anorexia, like a case of measles, runs its course.

Still others insist on therapy that involves the family as well. Indeed, the child psychiatrist Minuchin (1974) is convinced that family therapy is the *only* treatment for the anorexic. The therapist, according to Minuchin, becomes the leader of the family system and challenges the family's relationships. Particularly he reveals the interactions that have established enmeshment, overprotection, conflict avoidance, rigidity, and conflict-detouring. Family therapy provides a forceful way to disengage the overprotective family and to break up intensely symbiotic relationships.

Generally, family therapy is most effective when the patient is young, and when the illness is recent enough that a chronic state has not developed. Minuchin, however, is convinced that regardless of the circumstances, family treatment is effective in 86 percent of the cases, and that with family treatment anorexic symptoms disappear within two to eight weeks. Monthly sessions seldom exceed ten months. For him, interpersonal family relationships are the key.

I cannot speak for a therapy style that I have not experienced. For cases of anorexia that originate in adulthood, husband-wife therapy would seem useful for married patients. In my own situation, the conjugal environment was the most problematic subject to tackle in therapy. Anorexia nervosa does not occur in solitide, and those around an anorexic must be involved in therapy too.

Bruch (1978) is not convinced that family therapy is the treatment of choice, but she does insist that "The development of anorexia nervosa is so closely related to abnormal patterns of family interaction that successful treatment must always involve resolution of underlying family problems, which may not be identifiable as open conflicts; on the contrary, quite often excessive closeness and over-intense involvements lie at the roots" (p. 86). Whether through family or individual therapy, these problems deserve attention and understanding.

Behavioral methods of therapy have also been tested in

anorexia. Such programs are currently in progress at the University of Minnesota Hospitals; at the University of California, Los Angeles, Neuropsychiatric Institute; at the University of Nebraska Medical Center; and at other clinics. One approach is to offer exercise only as a reward for weight gain, a technique which often results in rapid weight increase. But the patient is gaining under duress and often does not change deeply engrained behavior patterns. So she immediately short-circuits the gain once she is released from the hospital. It is difficult to obtain long-term improvement unless the therapy pays attention to the reinforcement contingencies of the dieting itself.

Behaviorists join humanists, Gestaltists, and psychoanalysts in advocating the practice of avoided behaviors: that is, teaching new patterns of thought and behavior that her own rigid lifestyle kept her from perceiving. Exercises that guide the patient in distinguishing between "anorexic" and "appropriate" behavior are helpful. Even after the anorexic is committed to change, old behaviors in eating may persist, and so instruction in new patterns of behavior may be welcomed. She learns that she is not in control of her behavior until she can actually choose whether to eat anorexically or normally.

Behavioral treatment can also include homework assignments that give the patient practice in self-initiated activity, decision-making, and assertiveness with family and peers. These activities allow the patient to build positively reinforcing patterns in small increments, apart from the exclusive domain of weight.

For in anorexia nervosa, the girl has a very limited repertoire of positive reinforcers. Most revolve around the pleasures of weight loss and self-control. Weight gain is a negative reinforcer: so anorexic avoidance must be eliminated if possible, and certainly minimized. She needs to break the enslaving habit of constant weigh-ins, that time-consuming, panic-producing ritual that entraps the anorexic.

The anorexic needs to develop a gamut of new activities that offer pleasure. At first this task will be hard for one who judgmentally equates pleasure with frivolity and who gets satisfaction only from superior performance, often through suffering.

Once the anorexic will cooperate in setting goals, behavioral modification therapy can get underway. As noted earlier, occasionally the patient will gain rapidly to get out of the hospital, only to succumb to almost suicidal depression and rapid weight loss at home. However, if she participates in setting small, incremental goals, she is less likely to bolt and panic. She can be taught not to fear foods that she has long labelled "unacceptable," and to plan for larger consumption of food. By practicing these operations, the girl retains a sense of that all-important control.

Whatever the theory, beneficial therapy has to result in the attainment of a normal weight for the anorexic. Generally this is the weight at which menses are re-established and will probably be three to five pounds within the standard weight established for her body build and age. This weight must be achieved and *maintained*. Maintenance of desired weight can be a problem of long duration and may become critical for several years after therapy, at crisis points in her life. But even when she desires to gain an acceptable amount of weight, the anorexic panics at two points: one, when she initially gains weight; and two, as she approaches the critical weight for the menses to return. She may try to bargain with the therapist for a lower weight goal. But it cannot be a negotiable item, for if the patient once wheedles the agreement down to a lower weight, it starts a pattern in a downward spiral.

Weight gain is critical to an anorexic's recovery, both psychologically and physiologically. Emotional health cannot recur in a starvation state. The entire issue is landmined with pitfalls. Some advocate keeping the weight issue in the hands of the physician, so that gaining does not become the therapeutic issue. On the other hand it can be argued that when the physical and mental elements of the illness are separated, the treatment further dichotomizes the problem. If the therapist can establish a supportive, non-adversary role early, he or she will better be able to work with the issue of weight gain as well as its emotional connotation. The anorexic has already been battling extreme pressure to gain weight from parents, family, or spouse. She will not be receptive to additional sources of pressure.

Some researchers also advocate bibliotherapy, a process of

reading about others in similar situations and following their unraveling of the problem. Bruch's *Golden Cage*, Crisp's *Let Me Be*, or Liu's *Solitaire* are useful books in anorexia therapy. If the patient has the background to read with understanding, more technical works are acceptable too. Reading helps to discourage that sense of uniqueness, of being the only one with this problem—a quality of anorexia nervosa that is so appealing to the anorexic.

In conclusion, some facts bear reiteration on the subject of therapy in the treatment of anorexia nervosa. First, it should be remembered that despite the many similarities among anorexics, each case is individual. Universal explanations for causation and universal treatments can not be assumed.

Second, starvation promotes aberrant mental processes. The anorexic's physical condition must be improved before meaningful therapy can occur. There seems to be no statistical proof that hospitalization is preferable to out-patient treatment or vice versa, unless life is threatened.

Third, therapy may be cognitive, affective, or behavioral in design, but the most effective mode seems to be a combination. Whatever form, a trusting relationship between therapist and patient must be established. Therapy may or may not involve the family, but the faulty family interactions must be addressed. Effective therapy may take a long time, but it should not be terminated until the maladaptive behaviors are replaced by more positive actions.

Fourth, the anorexic must learn and *believe* that she has worth of her own and that she can and must listen to her own needs. Expectations of super-human performance become an impossible dictator to live under.

If these bewildered, self-hating girls can learn to accept imperfections in themselves, acknowledge faults in their parents, and accept pleasure as a real part of their lives, then the demon will be laid to rest.

Pain has an element of blank;
It cannot recollect
When it began, or if there were
A day when it was not.

It has no future but itself,
Its infinite realms contain
Its past, enlightened to perceive
New periods of pain.

—Emily Dickinson, *XIX*

Epilogue

It has taken me painful years to realize that parents—though deeply loved—can be wrong, that love can be smothering, and that a family's basic belief system may not encompass the different perceptions of a child. I still struggle at age 40 against the ingrained idea that "one does what one must," an unspoken motto in our household when I was growing up. When one lives by that motto, it becomes difficult to separate one's own feelings and notions, often based on one's own experience, from the framework of feelings and notions by which the family lives. Where does the separate person begin? How can I be a worthy individual if I don't receive constant affirmation from my family. This tumultuous conflict is an intense source of pain. The web of family interaction needs to be disengaged, tentacle by tentacle, and replaced with supportive distancing.

Even now as I write I feel guilty, wondering whether, by undergoing the profound transformation that I write about, I have hurt those I love deeply. Have I threatened others' self-worth? If I pull away and shout for space, will I create an abyss where others dear to me will tumble? I have been away a long time. Those I left behind functioned quite well without me. I fear lest my statement now in words is too strong; yet God knows the silent scream of anorexia is louder still.

At one point in my illness I feared that I was rebelling against God. But now it seems to me that it is not God I am disavowing but the elements of my childhood that were closely linked with God. If I can yank free of the ties that remain and land panting and sweating on my feet, I may be able finally to accept Him on my own. At last I think I will acknowledge the source of my anger. It is the god who failed: not God, but the system of values that I relied on way too much for support, which wasn't there when I most needed it, during the heart of the crisis. When I opposed all that I was conditioned to see as correct and moral and valued, there was nothing left for me to turn to for guidance, no inner resources, no rules independently derived. When change finally happened, I ripped away at myself like a frenzied gold seeker digging for the buried trove, hell-bent on discovering what was at my core. My body was just the outer layer of something deep within. I had never helped formulate those forces within, but they held the power to suffocate. It's a rather savage business.

It seems to me that the family unit has borne the brunt of the blame for the anorexic's condition. Certain psychoanalytically derived evidence supports this contention, but I think it is only fair to try to put the family relationship into some sort of perspective.

Anorexics have so many of the same symptoms of this disease— yet the suffering is an intensely personal experience. Perhaps from her deep pain the anorexic learns at last to heed her own internal signals and distinguish *her* needs from her family's. It is no longer enough to look to others to tell her how she feels. And after looking deeply into my own life, it seems to me that my family's net of interaction was woven with the strands of love.

I imagine such is the case in every anorexic's family. If, indeed, the anorexic has been too well-nourished with parental concern and over-fed on pride in her own stellar behavior, still parents have not done so maliciously. They know not what they do.

I was—and am—a daughter, but I'm nobody's little girl any more. At age 40 it is long past time to recognize that we all have chinks in our armor, but we need not be dismayed.

I am also a mother. And frankly, I am scared as hell that my great love for my daughters may be subverting their development. Who can predict? For now, I make a studied effort to bid them farewell as they go. I tell them to have a good time, rather than to be careful—and hope the understanding I have gained so painfully is theirs already.

Amid the convolutions of my life I have discovered that I am still visible and it feels very good.

BIBLIOGRAPHY

Bibliography

Anderson, A. E. in: "Anorexia the Starving Disease Epidemic." *U.S. News and World Report*, August 30, 1982, pp. 47–48.

Asbeck, F.; Hirschmann, W. D.; Deck, K.; and Castrup, H. J., "Lethal Course of Anorexia Nervosa: Alcohol and Laxative Abuse in a Female Patient." *Internist*. Berlin (1972), 63–65.

Binswanger, L. "Der Fall Ellen West." Schweiz: *Archives Neurological Psychiatry* 54 (1944), 69–117.

Boyar, R. M. et al. "Anorexia Nervosa: Immaturity of the 24-Hour Luteinizing Hormone Secretary Pattern." *New England Journal of Medicine* 291 (1974), 861–865.

Browning, C. H. and Miller, S. I. "Anorexia Nervosa: A Study in Prognosis and Management." *American Journal of Psychiatry* 124 (1968), 1128.

Brozek, J.; Wells, S.; and Keys, A., "Medical Aspects of Semi-starvation in Leningrad." *American Review of Soviet Medicine* 4 (1946), 70–79.

Bruch, H. "Eating Disorders of Adolescence." A paper in: *The Psychopathology of Adolescence*. Edited by Stanley Schachter. New York: Columbia University Press, 1969.

———— "Anorexia Nervosa and Its Treatment." *Journal of Pediatric Psychiatry* 2 (1977), 110–112.

———— "Family Transactions in Eating Disorders." *Comprehensive Psychiatry* 12 (1971), 238–248.

———— "Instinct and Interpersonal Experience." *Comprehensive Psychiatry* 11 (1970), 495–506.

———— Eating Disorders: *Obesity, Anorexia Nervosa and the Person Within*. New York: Basic Books, 1973b.

———— *The Golden Cage: The Enigma of Anorexia Nervosa.* Cambridge, Massachusetts: Harvard University Press, 1978.

———— *"Psychological Antecedents of Anorexia Nervosa." Anorexia Nervosa.* Edited by R. Vigersky. New York: Raven Press, 1979.

Crisp, A. H. "The Possible Significance of Some Behavior Correlates of Weight and Carbohydrate Intake." *Journal of Psychosomatic Research* 11 (1967), 117–131.

———— "Anorexia Nervosa: 'Feeding Disorder,' 'Nervous Malnutrition,' or 'Weight Phobia?'" *World Review Nutrition Diet* 12 (1970), 452–504.

———— "Diagnosis and Outcome of Anorexia Nervosa: The St. George's View." *Proceedings of the Royal Society of Medicine.* 70 (1977b), 686–690.

———— *Anorexia Nervosa: Let Me Be.* London Academic Press, 1980.

Crisp, A. H.; Harding, B.; and McGuiness, B., "Anorexia Nervosa: Psychoneurotic Characteristics of Parents: Relationship to Prognosis: A Quantitative Study." *Journal of Psychosomatic Research* 18 (1974), 167–173.

Crisp, A. H.; Kalucy, R. S.; Lacey, J. H.; and Harding, B., "The Long-Term Prognosis in Anorexia Nervosa: Some Factors Predictive of Outcome." *Anorexia Nervosa.* Edited by R. Vigersky. New York: Raven Press, 1977a.

Crisp, A. H.; Palmer, R. L.; and Kalucy, R. S., "How Common Is Anorexia Nervosa? A Prevalence Study." *British Journal of Psychiatry* 128 (1976), 549–554.

Crisp, A. H. and Toms, D. A., "Primary Anorexia Nervosa or Weight Phobia in the Male: Report on 13 Cases." *British Medical Journal* 1 (1972), 334.

Dally, P. *Anorexia Nervosa.* New York: Greene and Stratton, 1969.

Dally, P. and Gomez, J. *Anorexia Nervosa.* London: Heinemann, 1979.

Escalona, S. K., "Patterns of Infantile Experience and the Developmental Process." *Psychoanal. Study of the Child* 18 (1963), 197.

Falstein, E. I.; Sherman, D.; Feinstein, S. C.; and Judas, I., "Anorexia Nervosa in the Male Child." *American Journal of Orthopsychiatry* 26 (1956), 751–772.

Feighner, J. P.; Robins, E.; Guzer, S. B., et al., "Diagnostic Criteria for Use in Psychiatric Research." *Archives of General Psychiatry* 26 *1* (1972), 57.

Freud, S. "Recommendations for Physicians on the Psychoanalytic Method for Treatment" (1912). *Standard Edition* 12. London: Hogarth Press (1957), 109–120.

Garfinkel, P and Garner, D. *Anorexia Nervosa: A Multidimensional Perspective.* New York: Brunner/Mazel, 1982.

Gull, W. W. *Anorexia Nervosa.* Translated by Clinical Society (London), 7 (1874), 22–28. Reprinted in: *Evolution of Psychosomatic Concepts. Anorexia Nervosa: A Paradigm.* Edited by R. M. Kaufman and M. Heiman. New York: International Universities Press, 1964.

Halmi, K. A.; Dekirmenjian, H.; Davis, J. M.; Casper, R.; and Goldberg, S., "Catecholamine Metabolism in Anorexia Nervosa." *Archives of General Psychiatry* 35 (1978), 458–460.

Hebb, D. O. *Organization of Behavior.* New York: Wiley, 1949.

Janet, P. *The Major Symptoms of Hysteria.* New York: Macmillan, 1929.

Jessner, L. and Abse, D. W. "Regressive Forces in Anorexia Nervosa." *British Journal of Medical Psychology* 33 (1960), 301–312.

Keys, A.; Brozek, J.; Henschel, A.; Mickelson, O.; and Taylor, H., *The Biology of Human Starvation* II. Minneapolis: University of Minnesota Press, 1950.

Kubie, L. S. "Multiple Fallacies in the Concept of Schizophrenia." *Journal of Nervous Mental Disorders* 153 (1971), 331–342.

Lasèque, C. "De L'Anorexie Hystérique." *Arch. Gen. de Med.* 385 (1973). Reprinted in *Evolution of Psychosomatic Concepts. Anorexia Nervosa: A Paradigm.* Edited by R. M. Kaufman and M. Heiman. New York: International Universities Press, 1964.

Levenkron, S. *The Best Little Girl in the World.* Wakefield, Maryland: Contemporary Books, 1978.

Mahler, M. S. "On the Significance of the Normal Separation—Individuation Phase." In: *Drives, Affects, Behavior.* New York: International University Press, 1965.

Minuchin, S.; Baker, L.; Rosman, B. L.; Liebman, R.; Milman, L.; and Todd, T. C., "A Conceptual Model of Psychosomatic Illness in Children. Family Organization and Family Therapy." *Archives of General Psychiatry* 32 (1975), 1031–1038.

Minuchin, S.; Rosman, B. L.; and Baker, L., *Psychosomatic Families: Anorexia Nervosa in Context.* Cambridge, Massachusetts: Harvard University Press, 1978.

Moldofsky, H. and Garfinkel, P. E. "Problems of Treatment of Anorexia Nervosa." *Canadian Psychiatric Association Journal* 19 (1974), 169–175.

Morton, R. *Phthisiologica: Or a Treatise of Consumptions.* London: S. Smith and B. Walford, 1964.

Moulton, R. "A Psychosomatic Study of Anorexia Nervosa Including the Use of Vaginal Smears." *Psychosomatic Medicine* 4 (1942), 62–74.

Piaget, J. *The Construction of Reality in the Child.* New York: Basic Books, 1954.

Pierloot, R. A.; Wellens, W.; and Houben, M. E., "Elements of Resistance to a Combined Medical and Psychotherapeutic Program in Anorexia Nervosa: An Overview." *Psychotherapy and Psychosomatics 26 (1976), 101–117.*

Ross, J. L. *Anorexia Nervosa: An Overview.* Bulletin of the Menninger Clinic 41 (1977), 418–436.

Russell, G. F. M. "Metabolic Aspects of Anorexia Nervosa." *Proceedings of the Royal Society of Medicine* 58 (1965), 811–814.

——— "General Management of Anorexia Nervosa and Difficulties in Assessing the Efficacy of Treatment." In: *Anorexia Nervosa.* Edited by R. Vigersky. New York: Raven Press, 1979.

Selvini-Palazzoli, M. P. *Self-Starvation.* London: Chaucer Publishing Co., 1974.

Silverstone, K. T. "Appetite and Food Intake, Report of the Dahlem Workshop on Appetite and Food Intake." In: *Life Science Research Reports* II. Berlin, 1975.

Simmonds, M. "Über Embolische Prozesse in des Hypophysis." *Arch. J. Pat. Anat.* 217 (1914), 226–239.

Spitz, R. A. *The First Year of Life.* New York: International University Press, 1965.

Sours, J. A. *Starving to Death in a Sea of Objects: The Anorexia Nervosa Syndrome.* New York: Aronson, 1980.

——— "Starving Amid Plenty." *Science Digest*, July, 1981, p. 56.

Szyrynski, V. "Anorexia Nervosa and Psychotherapy." *American Journal of Psychotherapy* 27 (1973), 492–505.

Thoma, H. *Anorexia Nervosa.* Translated by G. Brydone. New York: International Universities Press, 1967.

Walter, J. V.; Kaufman, M. R.; and Deutsche, F., "Anorexia Nervosa: Psychosomatic Entity." *Psychosomatic Medicine* 2 (1940), 3–16.

Weiner, H. *Psychobiology and Human Disease.* New York: Elsevier, North Holland, Inc., 1977.

Woodman, M. *The Owl Was a Baker's Daughter.* Toronto: Inner City Books, 1980.